# First World War
### and Army of Occupation
# War Diary
### France, Belgium and Germany

35 DIVISION
105 Infantry Brigade
Gloucestershire Regiment
14th (Service) Battalion (West of England)
31 January 1916 - 14 February 1918

WO95/2488/1

Published by

## The Naval & Military Press Ltd

Unit 10 Ridgewood Industrial Park,

Uckfield, East Sussex,

TN22 5QE England

Tel: +44 (0) 1825 749494

www.naval-military-press.com

www.nmarchive.com

*This diary has been reprinted in facsimile from the original. Any imperfections are inevitably reproduced and the quality may fall short of modern type and cartographic standards.*

© **Crown Copyright**
**Images reproduced by permission of The National Archives, London, England, 2015.**

# Contents

| Document type | Place/Title | Date From | Date To |
|---|---|---|---|
| Heading | WO95/2488/1 14 Battalion Gloucestershire. Regiment | | |
| Heading | 35th Division 105th Infy Bde 14th Bn Gloster Regt Jan 1916-Feb 1918 Dis Banded | | |
| Heading | 35 14th Gloucester Vol I | | |
| War Diary | Havre | 31/01/1916 | 02/02/1916 |
| War Diary | Blondecque | 03/02/1916 | 03/02/1916 |
| War Diary | Ebblingham | 09/02/1916 | 09/02/1916 |
| War Diary | Mollinghem | 19/02/1916 | 19/02/1916 |
| War Diary | Robecq | 20/02/1916 | 20/02/1916 |
| War Diary | La Pannarie | 20/02/1916 | 29/02/1916 |
| Heading | War Diary. 14th (Service) Battalion Gloucestershire Regiment. Period 1st March 1916 To 31st March 1916 14 Gloucesterr Vol 2 | | |
| War Diary | Le Touret | 01/03/1916 | 07/03/1916 |
| War Diary | Robecqe | 08/03/1916 | 08/03/1916 |
| War Diary | Colonne | 09/03/1916 | 19/03/1916 |
| War Diary | Les Lobes | 20/03/1916 | 25/03/1916 |
| War Diary | Estaires | 25/03/1916 | 26/03/1916 |
| War Diary | Laventie | 27/03/1916 | 12/04/1916 |
| War Diary | Sailly | 13/04/1916 | 19/04/1916 |
| War Diary | La Couture | 19/04/1916 | 06/05/1916 |
| War Diary | Vielle Chapelle | 07/05/1916 | 14/05/1916 |
| War Diary | Croix Barbee | 15/05/1916 | 30/05/1916 |
| War Diary | ? Chapelle | 30/05/1916 | 09/06/1916 |
| War Diary | Croix Barbee | 10/06/1916 | 15/06/1916 |
| War Diary | Vielle Chapelle | 16/06/1916 | 16/06/1916 |
| War Diary | Hingette | 17/06/1916 | 30/06/1916 |
| War Diary | 14th. (Service) Battalion Gloucestershire Regiment. | 30/05/1916 | 30/05/1916 |
| Miscellaneous | Full Report Of Raid on the night of 8th. June 1916. | 08/06/1916 | 08/06/1916 |
| Heading | 105th Bde. 35th Div. War Diary 14th Battalion Gloucestershire Regiment. 1st to 31st July 1916 | | |
| War Diary | Hingette | 01/07/1916 | 03/07/1916 |
| War Diary | Lucheux | 03/07/1916 | 06/07/1916 |
| War Diary | Beauval | 07/07/1916 | 09/07/1916 |
| War Diary | Bus | 10/07/1916 | 10/07/1916 |
| War Diary | Warloy | 11/07/1916 | 13/07/1916 |
| War Diary | Bois-Les-Celestine | 14/07/1916 | 14/07/1916 |
| War Diary | Grove Tour | 15/07/1916 | 15/07/1916 |
| War Diary | Billon Wood | 16/07/1916 | 16/07/1916 |
| War Diary | Moricourt | 17/07/1916 | 31/07/1916 |
| Heading | 105th Brigade. 35th Division. 1/14th Battalion Gloucestershire Regiment August 1916 | | |
| War Diary | Sand Pit Valley | 01/08/1916 | 01/08/1916 |
| War Diary | Bois De Tailles | 02/08/1916 | 06/08/1916 |
| War Diary | Riencourt | 07/08/1916 | 10/08/1916 |
| War Diary | Citadel | 11/08/1916 | 19/08/1916 |
| War Diary | Lancaster & Dawson Trenches | 20/08/1916 | 20/08/1916 |
| War Diary | Lamb Trench Overflow Trench (Reserve) | 22/08/1916 | 22/08/1916 |
| War Diary | Lamb Trench | 23/08/1916 | 23/08/1916 |
| War Diary | Bronfay Farm. | 24/08/1916 | 25/08/1916 |

| | | | |
|---|---|---|---|
| War Diary | Sand Pit Valley | 26/08/1916 | 28/08/1916 |
| War Diary | Bois des Tailles | 29/08/1916 | 30/08/1916 |
| War Diary | Prouville | 31/08/1916 | 31/08/1916 |
| War Diary | Crouches | 01/09/1916 | 01/09/1916 |
| War Diary | Lucheux | 01/09/1916 | 01/09/1916 |
| War Diary | Agnez Les Duisans | 01/09/1916 | 02/09/1916 |
| War Diary | Arras. | 03/09/1916 | 16/09/1916 |
| War Diary | J.3. Sub Sector | 17/09/1916 | 23/09/1916 |
| War Diary | Arras | 24/09/1916 | 28/09/1916 |
| War Diary | J 2. Sub Sector. | 29/09/1916 | 30/09/1916 |
| War Diary | Arras | 01/10/1916 | 01/10/1916 |
| War Diary | Sub Sector. J.2. | 02/10/1916 | 09/10/1916 |
| War Diary | J.1. Sub Sector. | 10/10/1916 | 14/10/1916 |
| War Diary | Arras. | 15/10/1916 | 15/10/1916 |
| War Diary | J.1. Sub Sector | 16/10/1916 | 18/10/1916 |
| War Diary | Arras. | 19/10/1916 | 22/10/1916 |
| War Diary | J.3. Sub Sector | 23/10/1916 | 27/10/1916 |
| War Diary | Arras J.3 Sub Sector | 28/10/1916 | 31/10/1916 |
| War Diary | Arras. | 01/11/1916 | 03/11/1916 |
| War Diary | J.R. Sub Sector. | 03/11/1916 | 07/11/1916 |
| War Diary | J.II Sub Sector Arras | 08/11/1916 | 11/11/1916 |
| War Diary | Arras | 12/11/1916 | 14/11/1916 |
| War Diary | J.1. Sub Sec. | 15/11/1916 | 23/11/1916 |
| War Diary | Arras. | 24/11/1916 | 26/11/1916 |
| War Diary | J.2 Sub Sector. | 27/11/1916 | 30/11/1916 |
| War Diary | J.II Sub Sector | 28/11/1916 | 30/11/1916 |
| War Diary | Arras. J.2 Sub Sector. | 01/12/1916 | 03/12/1916 |
| War Diary | Duissans | 04/12/1916 | 04/12/1916 |
| War Diary | Manin-Givechy. Le Noble | 05/12/1916 | 28/12/1916 |
| War Diary | Arras | 28/12/1916 | 03/02/1917 |
| War Diary | Moncheaux | 04/02/1917 | 20/02/1917 |
| War Diary | Chilly | 21/02/1917 | 28/02/1917 |
| War Diary | Chilly Sector | 01/03/1917 | 07/03/1917 |
| War Diary | Decauville | 08/03/1917 | 14/03/1917 |
| War Diary | Lihons | 14/03/1917 | 23/03/1917 |
| War Diary | Curchy | 24/03/1917 | 31/03/1917 |
| War Diary | Hombleux | 01/04/1917 | 11/04/1917 |
| War Diary | Monchy-Lagache | 12/04/1917 | 15/04/1917 |
| War Diary | Gricourt | 16/04/1917 | 21/04/1917 |
| War Diary | Keepers Lodge | 22/04/1917 | 24/04/1917 |
| War Diary | Gricourt | 25/04/1917 | 30/04/1917 |
| War Diary | Villeveque | 01/05/1917 | 08/05/1917 |
| War Diary | Keepers Lodge. | 09/05/1917 | 13/05/1917 |
| War Diary | Gricourt | 14/05/1917 | 16/05/1917 |
| War Diary | Keepers Lodge | 17/05/1917 | 19/05/1917 |
| War Diary | Tertry | 20/05/1917 | 22/05/1917 |
| War Diary | Peronne | 23/05/1917 | 24/05/1917 |
| War Diary | Aizecourt-Le-Bas | 25/05/1917 | 31/05/1917 |
| Miscellaneous | To 105th Bde. | 08/07/1917 | 08/07/1917 |
| War Diary | Aizecourt-Le-Bas. | 01/06/1917 | 02/06/1917 |
| War Diary | Villers-Guislain | 03/06/1917 | 18/06/1917 |
| War Diary | Heudicourt | 19/06/1917 | 26/06/1917 |
| War Diary | Gauche-Wood | 26/06/1917 | 01/07/1917 |
| War Diary | Villers Faucon | 02/07/1917 | 07/07/1917 |
| War Diary | Ephey | 08/07/1917 | 15/07/1917 |
| War Diary | Aizecourt-Le-Bas. | 16/07/1917 | 22/07/1917 |

| | | | |
|---|---|---|---|
| War Diary | Lempire. | 22/07/1917 | 01/08/1917 |
| War Diary | Aizecourt Le-Bas | 02/08/1917 | 17/08/1917 |
| War Diary | Lempire | 18/08/1917 | 20/08/1917 |
| War Diary | Knoll | 21/08/1917 | 22/08/1917 |
| War Diary | Lempire | 23/08/1917 | 27/08/1917 |
| War Diary | Villers-Faucon | 28/08/1917 | 31/08/1917 |
| War Diary | Lempire | 01/09/1917 | 06/09/1917 |
| War Diary | St Emelie. | 07/09/1917 | 11/09/1917 |
| War Diary | Aizecourt Le-Bas. | 12/09/1917 | 18/09/1917 |
| War Diary | Epehy | 19/09/1917 | 30/09/1917 |
| War Diary | Villers Faucon. | 01/10/1917 | 01/10/1917 |
| War Diary | Peronne | 02/10/1917 | 03/10/1917 |
| War Diary | Arras. | 04/10/1917 | 04/10/1917 |
| War Diary | Dainville. | 05/10/1917 | 13/10/1917 |
| War Diary | Ledringhem | 14/10/1917 | 15/10/1917 |
| War Diary | Proven. | 16/10/1917 | 16/10/1917 |
| War Diary | Elverdinghe | 17/10/1917 | 18/10/1917 |
| War Diary | Houlthulst Forest. | 22/10/1917 | 22/10/1917 |
| War Diary | Elverdinghe | 19/10/1917 | 20/10/1917 |
| War Diary | Houlthulst Forest | 21/10/1917 | 21/10/1917 |
| War Diary | Larrey Camp. | 23/10/1917 | 29/10/1917 |
| War Diary | Houlthulst Forest | 30/10/1917 | 01/11/1917 |
| War Diary | Dykes Camp. | 02/11/1917 | 05/11/1917 |
| War Diary | Penton Camp | 06/11/1917 | 10/11/1917 |
| War Diary | Petworth Camp. | 11/11/1917 | 15/11/1917 |
| War Diary | 'Fa' 'X". Camp. | 16/11/1917 | 24/11/1917 |
| War Diary | Canal Bank | 25/11/1917 | 28/11/1917 |
| War Diary | Siege Camp. | 29/11/1917 | 29/11/1917 |
| War Diary | Siege Camp & Kempton Park. | 30/11/1917 | 30/11/1917 |
| War Diary | Kempton Park and Turco Camp | 01/12/1917 | 02/12/1917 |
| War Diary | Siege Camp | 03/12/1917 | 05/12/1917 |
| War Diary | Langemarck Sector | 06/12/1917 | 08/12/1917 |
| War Diary | Siege Camp | 09/12/1917 | 09/12/1917 |
| War Diary | Herzeele | 10/12/1917 | 11/12/1917 |
| War Diary | School Camp | 12/12/1917 | 02/01/1918 |
| War Diary | March Camp | 03/01/1918 | 09/01/1918 |
| War Diary | Canal Bank | 10/01/1918 | 16/01/1918 |
| War Diary | Left Sector | 17/01/1918 | 24/01/1918 |
| War Diary | Turco Camp | 25/01/1918 | 01/02/1918 |
| War Diary | Langemarck Sector | 02/02/1918 | 05/02/1918 |
| War Diary | Soult Camp | 06/02/1918 | 06/02/1918 |
| War Diary | Eagle Trench | 06/02/1918 | 08/02/1918 |
| War Diary | J. Camp | 09/02/1918 | 11/02/1918 |
| War Diary | Bollizelle | 12/02/1918 | 14/02/1918 |

WO/95/2488/1

14 Battalion Gloucestershire Regiment

35TH DIVISION
105TH INFY BDE

14TH BN GLOSTER REGT
~~JAN~~
~~FEB~~ 1916-FEB 1918

DISBANDED

35/14 Kh. Ghalib
Vol I

Army Form C. 2118.

10/35

Instructions regarding War Diaries and Intelligence
Summaries are contained in F. S. Regs., Part II.
and the Staff Manual respectively. Title pages
will be prepared in manuscript.

# WAR DIARY
or
# INTELLIGENCE SUMMARY.
(Erase heading not required.)

| Place | Date | Hour | Summary of Events and Information | Remarks and references to Appendices |
|---|---|---|---|---|
| Havre | 31-1-16 | 3 p.m. | Arrived. Landed at 7 a.m. Encamped at No 5 Rest Camp. AAA | |
| | 2-2-16 | 4 a.m. | Entrained. AAA | |
| Blondecque | 3-2-16 | 1 a.m. | Detrained. Marched to Eblinghem. (In Billets) AAA. | |
| Eblinghem | 9-2-16 | 7 a.m. | Marched to Mollinghem (In Billets) AAA | |
| Mollinghem | 19-2-16 | 8 a.m. | Marched to Robecq – Billeted on night AAA | |
| Robecq | 20-2-16 | 10 a.m. | Marched to La Pannerie – Detailed as Divl Reserve to 5th Division – In billets AAA | |
| La Pannerie | 20-2-16 | 11 p.m. | Received orders to Stand to Arms, Gas attack threatened. AAA | |
| | 21-2-16 | 1 a.m. | Received message, Danger over. dismiss men. AAA | |
| La Pannerie | 27-2-16 | 10 a.m. | Marched to LE TOURET. Attached to 115th Inf Bde for instruction in Trench Warfare. AAA W Coy attached to 16th Welch Regt. X Coy attached to 11th S.W.B. Y Coy to 10th S.W.B.'s AAA Z. Coy and Batt. H.Q. to 17th R.W.Fusiliers. AAA W and X Coys in 1st Line Trenches: X Coys close support at FESTUBERT. Z Coy in AAA Reserve at LE TOURET. AAA | |
| | 28-2-16 | | As for 27th AAA | |
| | 29-2-16 | | As for 28th AAA | |

E.L.Welch
Lieut Colonel
16 (S) 13 Battn  Chester Regiment

Bromley

14 Gloucesters Vol 2

# WAR DIARY.

## 14TH (SERVICE) BATTALION, GLOUCESTERSHIRE REGIMENT.

Period 1ST March 1916 to 31ST March 1916

# WAR DIARY
## or
## INTELLIGENCE SUMMARY.
(Erase heading not required.)

Army Form C. 2118.

| Place | Date | Hour | Summary of Events and Information | Remarks and references to Appendices |
|---|---|---|---|---|
| LE TOURET | 1-3-16 | | W and X Companies in 1st line Trenches, Y Company in Support at FESTUBERT. Z Company in reserve at LE TOURET. | |
| LE TOURET | 2-3-16 | 5.30 pm | W Coy in Reserve at LE TOURET, X Coy to Support at FESTUBERT. Y Coy to front line, Z Coy to front line. Two men killed: - buried in British Cemetery at LE TOURET. Same as for the 2nd inst. One Man Killed: - buried at LE TOURET. Three men wounded. | |
| | 3-3-16 | | As for 3rd. | |
| | 4-3-16 | | As for 4th. Received Operation Orders from 115th Bde ordering the Battn to return to Robecq on the 7th. One man wounded. | |
| | 5-3-16 | 5.30 pm | Changed Relief. W Coy to front line. X Coy to Support at Festubert. Z to Reserve at LE TOURET. One man died of wounds. | |
| | 6-3-16 | 4 am | All Coys evacuated their positions and concentrated at LE TOURET. One man accidentally wounded by Bomb explosion. | |
| | 7-3-16 | 8 a.m. | Three Hundred men returned to Robecq by Motor bus. The remainder marched. Climatic Conditions - very cold, during snow. | |
| Robecq | | 12 Noon | All Ranks billeted. Billets taken over from 15th Sherwood Foresters were in a clean and satisfactory condition. | |
| | 8-3-16 | | In billets. 2 Officers 100 Other Ranks proceeded to Rifle Range at K.25.6 - K.26.a.(5,34a) as Working Party. Billeting Party sent to Colonne to arrange billets for Battn. | |
| Colonne | 9-3-16 | 10.30 am | Marched to Colonne. all ranks billeted by 11.20 am. | |
| | 10-3-16 | 9.30 am | Tactical Working Party of Two Officers 100 Other Ranks sent to R.18.a.7.3. under C.R.E. 35th Division. Working Party of One Officer and 60 Other Ranks sent to Q.6.d.6.6. to erect Snipers Range. | |
| | 11-3-16 | 8 am | Working Party consisting of all Ranks W Coy reg. to R.18.a.7.3. Working party reported from Rifle Range at K.25.13. | |
| | | 10 a.m. | 1 Officer Two N.C.O.'s Incidental to Vickers on Course of Inst in Vickers M.G. (4 bass.) Two Platoons X Coy furnished Working Party at 8 Sec. 66. as Personnel for Trench Mortar Battery. Party of 1 Officer and 16 other Ranks proceeded to 105th Bde H.Q. | |
| | 12-3-16 | 8 am | Working Party consisting of Y½ Coy full strength proceeded to LE MAIRIAS GROUP, under Lt Turner. 1st Siege Coy. | |
| | 13-3-16 | 8 am | 120 all Ranks X Coy furnished Tactical Working Party at CARTERS POST. W Coy furnished 50 all Ranks at PONT RIQUEUZ, and 120 men at CLIFTON Group. | |
| | 14-3-16 | | Y Coy furnished Working Party at Carters Post; Z Coy Clifton Group. W Coy Pont Riqueuz. Two men proceeded to Aire on Course of Inst in ANTI GAS. | |
| | 15-3-16 | | Z Coy full strength proceeded to LE VERTBOIS to carry out MUSKETRY | |

Eleut. Col.
Comdg. 14th (S) Bn. Gloster Regt. (W. of E.)

Army Form C. 2118.

# WAR DIARY
of
## INTELLIGENCE SUMMARY.
(Erase heading not required.)

Instructions regarding War Diaries and Intelligence Summaries are contained in F.S. Regs., Part II. and the Staff Manual respectively. Title pages will be prepared in manuscript.

| Place | Date | Hour | Summary of Events and Information | Remarks and references to Appendices |
|---|---|---|---|---|
| Calonne | 16/3/16 | 8 a.m. | X Coy and Y Coy furnished a Tactical Working Party of 200 men at LE MARAIS R.16.C.9.8. W Coy furnished a working party of 50 men at Pont Riquel. R.9.C.8.4. | |
| | 17.3.16 | — | Ordinary Routine in Billets. | |
| | 18.3.16 | — | Ordinary Routine in Billets. Received 105th Bde Order No 10 Copy 5. ordering move to new billets on 19th inst | |
| | 19.3.16 | 9.30am | Marched via Quentin to LES LOBES. | |
| LES LOBES | 20.3.16 | — | In Billets | |
| | 21.3.16 | 8 a.m. | Officers Patrols sent out to reconnoitre all Defensive Positions within four mile radius of Point R.3.2.C.9.2. | |
| | | 9 a.m. | Tactical Working Party 75 all ranks sent to Pt X.17.d. to work under C.R.A. | |
| | | 12 noon | | |
| | | 4 p.m. | | |
| | | 4 p.m. | Received 105th BDE Order No 11 Copy 6. giving orders for the Relief of 100th BDE by 105th Bde at AUCHY. | |
| — | 22nd | 8 a.m. | Message received cancelling 105th 13de Order No 11 dated 21-3-16. | |
| — | 23 | — | In Billets. | |
| — | 24 | 8 a.m. | Comdg Officer and four Officers Comdg Coys proceeded by car from 105th 13DE H.Q. to want new line of trenches. | |
| | | 10 a.m. | Received Orders from 105th Bde to march to ESTAIRE on the 25th to be clear of presentbillets by 2:30 p.m. | |
| | | 12 noon | Billets. Your proceeded to new Billeting area. | |
| | 25 | 4.30 pm | Received 105 Bn Order No 12 Copy No 6 Containing particulars of the Relief of the 23rd Bde by the 105th 13de at LAVENTIE. Also march table for move to ESTAIRES on the 25th | |
| ESTAIRES | 25 | 1.34 pm | Marched independently to ESTAIRES. | |
| | | 4.30pm | Billetts for the night. | |

G.C.R...
Lieut. Col.
Comdg. 14th (ST) Bn. Gloster Regt. (W. of E.)

Army Form C. 2118.

# WAR DIARY
## or
## INTELLIGENCE SUMMARY.
*(Erase heading not required.)*

Instructions regarding War Diaries and Intelligence Summaries are contained in F. S. Regs., Part II. and the Staff Manual respectively. Title pages will be prepared in manuscript.

| Place | Date | Hour | Summary of Events and Information | Remarks and references to Appendices |
|---|---|---|---|---|
| ESTAIRES | 26.3.16 | 10 a.m. | Machine Gun (Brigade) moved into the Trenches at LAVENTIE. | |
| | | 5 p.m. | The Battalion concentrated at Point G.26.c.4.3 (Sheet 36) and marched via LE NAUMOND to LAVENTIE. The Transport moved independently; When moving along the SAILLY - LAVENTIE Rd Coys moved at 10 min interval. | |
| | | 6 p.m. | All Ranks were billeted and returned for the following day; W.Coy furnished the Garrison for EN an Post LAVENTIE EAST strength Two Platoons, and PECANTIN strength One Platoon. X Coy furnished Garrison for DEAD END, strength One Platoon. | |
| LAVENTIE | 27.3.16 | | Operations in the Posts held by the Battn Nil. Repair and Improvements of Posts proceeded with. | |
| " | 28.3.16 | | Operations Nil :- Intelligence :- An English Aeroplane was seen flying between LAVENTIE and Two Batteries East of the Post LAVENTIE EAST: O.C. the Post adopted that it might be an English Plane captured by the Germans as its manoeuvres are peculiar. Work of Repair proceeded with. | |
| " | 29 | 2:30 p.m. | Work of Repair proceeded with; PICONTIN POST heavily shelled by the enemy; No damage to Post. One man slightly wounded. | |
| " | 30 | 7 p.m. | Relieved 15th Cheshires in LEFT Sub-Section FAUQUISSART SECTION. The Relief was completed by 10:15 p.m. During the night of 30 - 31st both our own and Enemy M. G. were very active. The Snipers were also very active. | |
| " | 31 | -- | Enemy Snipers active up to 12 Noon. Since then have been very quiet. Enemy reported carrying out extensive work in front line trenches. Situation normal. | |

A. Walker
Lieut. Col.
Comdg. 12th (S) Bn. Gloster Regt. (W. of E.)

April May June
14 Gloucesters
Vols. 3.4.5

Army Form C. 2118.

# WAR DIARY
or
## INTELLIGENCE SUMMARY.
(Erase heading not required.)

| Place | Date | Hour | Summary of Events and Information | Remarks and references to Appendices |
|---|---|---|---|---|
| Levantie | 1-4-16 | | Snipers on both sides very active. Our Snipers claim two victims. Very little Enemy M.G. during night of 1-2. Several enemy working parties discovered & dispersed by M.G. fire. | |
| — | 2-4-16 | | Enemy working parties were extremely busy on their wire and Parapets. All dispersed time after time by M.G. fire. | |
| — | 3-4-16 | | A combined Artillery, Trench Mortar and M.G. minor operation was ordered. Our Artillery opened an intense bombardment of Enemy front line & Communication trenches at 6.45 p.m. lasting 5 minutes. M.G's and Trench Mortars then opened fire lasting for 15 minutes. The enemy retaliated with a heavy bombardment of our front line but no damage was done. Continuous M.G. fire was kept up by both sides during the night. | |
| | 4-4-16 | | Raining last 24 hours. Enemy Snipers have shewn little activity. During the night Hostile M.G. frequently traversed our Parapet. We vigorously replied. | |
| | 5-4-16 | 9 p.m. | The day passed quietly. The Battalion was relieved from the front Line trenches at 9 p.m. by the 13th Cheshires. The relief was carried out without incident. LEVANTIE EAST. Two Platoons 'B' Support Posts were occupied by the Bath as follows:- PICANTIN Post:- One Platoon. HUGOMONT Post:- One Platoon. DEAD END Post:- One Platoon. JOCK'S LODGE (by night):- One Section. The Remainder of the Bath in Billets on LEVANTIE. | |
| | 6/4/16 | — | The whole of the Bath in Billets employed on R.E. Working Parties at various parts of the line. | |
| | 7/4/16 | — | Ditto. | |
| | 8/4/16 | 4.30 p.m | Ditto up to 4.30 p.m. Relieved 15 Batt. Cheshire Regt in the Front Line. Relief completed by 9.30 p.m. | |
| | 9-4-16 | — | The day passed quietly. M.G's on both sides were active throughout the night of 8-9. | |
| | 10-4-16 | — | No change. Intermittent exchanges of Rifle and M.G. fire. | |

A.H. Radcliffe

Army Form C. 2118.

# WAR DIARY
## or
## INTELLIGENCE SUMMARY.
*(Erase heading not required.)*

Instructions regarding War Diaries and Intelligence Summaries are contained in F. S. Regs., Part II. and the Staff Manual respectively. Title pages will be prepared in manuscript.

| Place | Date | Hour | Summary of Events and Information | Remarks and references to Appendices |
|---|---|---|---|---|
| AVENTE | 11/4/16 | — | Enemy Snipers almost totally inactive during the whole of the day. At 8 p.m. on the night of the 10th a Minor Operation took place against the Enemy Artillery M.G. Trench. Mortar and Infantry took part. The operation took place at 8.30 p.m and was kept up until 10 p.m. The enemy replied but feebly. | |
| — | 12/4/16 | 10 p.m. | Relieved from Front Line Trenches by 17th Westyorks. Marched to billets at Sailly. | |
| Sailly | 13/4/16 | — | The Battn detailed as 35th Div Reserve. In Billets. | |
| | 14/4/16 | — | Ditto. Reinforcing Draft of 19 men arrived. | |
| | 15/4/16 | — | Ditto | |
| | 16/4/16 | — | Ditto | |
| | 17/4/16 | — | Ditto | |
| | 18/4/16 | 10.15 am | Marched to Fosse. In billets by 2 p.m. | |
| | 19/4/16 | 10.30 am | Marched to LACOUTURE. In billets on King's Road. Relieved 6 Wilts as Right Reserve Bn in the Ferme Du Bois Section. | |
| LACOUTURE | — | — | 105th Bde Reserve. | |
| — | 20/4/16 | — | Ditto | |
| — | 21/4/16 | — | Ditto | |
| — | 22/4/16 | — | Ditto | |
| — | 23/4/16 | — | Relieved 15 Sherwood Foresters in Front Line Trenches (Ferme du Bois). | |

# WAR DIARY
## INTELLIGENCE SUMMARY.
(Erase heading not required.)

Army Form C. 2118.

Instructions regarding War Diaries and Intelligence Summaries are contained in F.S. Regs., Part II. and the Staff Manual respectively. Title pages will be prepared in manuscript.

| Places | Date | Hour | Summary of Events and Information | Remarks and references to Appendices |
|---|---|---|---|---|
| LACOUTURE | 24/4/16 | — | Battalion in Front Line FERME DU BOIS | |
| | 25/4/16 | — | Ditto | |
| | 26/4/16 | — | Ditto | |
| | 27/4/16 | — | Ditto :- Relieved by 15th SHERWOODS at 10.15 p.m. | |
| | 28/4/16 | — | Batn in Bde Reserve :- | |
| | 29/4/16 | — | Ditto | |
| | 30/4/16 | — | Ditto | |
| | 1/5/16 | — | Ditto | |
| | 2/5/16 | — | Ditto | |
| | 3/5/16 | — | Relieved by 17th Bn Royal Scots. Relieved 15th Sherwoods in Front Line (Ferme Du Bois) | |
| | 4/5/16 | — | Battalion in Front Line (Ferme Du Bois). | |
| | 5/5/16 | — | Ditto | |
| | 6/5/16 | — | Ditto up to 10.40 p.m. Relieved by 17th Royal Scots:- Marched to Vielle Chapelle | |
| Vielle Chapelle | 7/5/16 | — | In Divisional Reserve at Vielle Chapelle. | |
| | 8/5/16 | — | Ditto | |
| | 9/5/16 | — | Ditto | |
| | 10/5/16 | — | Ditto | |
| | 11/5/16 | — | Ditto | |
| | 12/5/16 | — | Ditto | |
| | 13/5/16 | — | Ditto; Received orders to relieve 20th Lanc. Fusiliers in Neuve Chapelle Section on 14 inst | A. Caroline |

Army Form C. 2118.

# WAR DIARY
## or
## INTELLIGENCE SUMMARY.
(Erase heading not required.)

Instructions regarding War Diaries and Intelligence Summaries are contained in F.S. Regs., Part II. and the Staff Manual respectively. Title pages will be prepared in manuscript.

| Place | Date | Hour | Summary of Events and Information | Remarks and references to Appendices |
|---|---|---|---|---|
| Nex Chapelle | 14-5-16 | 8.30pm | Relieved 20th Lancs Fusiliers in Neuve Chapelle Section (Front Line) | |
| Croix Barbee | 15-5-16 to 18-5-16 | | In Front Line - Neuve Chapelle. Relieved by 15th Sherwoods at 8.30 p.m. 18-5-16. | |
| | 19th | | Battn. in Brigade Reserve at Croix Barbee - Relieved 15th Sherwoods on 22-5-16 in Front Line | |
| | 20. 21. | | Front Line - Neuve Chapelle. Relieved by Sherwoods at 8.30 p.m. 25-5-16. | |
| | 22. 23. 24. 25. | | | |
| | 26-5-16 | | Bn. Reserve - Croix Barbee | |
| | 27.5.16 | | Ditto | |
| | 28.5.16 | | Ditto | |
| | 29.5.16 | | Ditto | |
| | 30.5.16 | 8.30pm | Enemy after Heavy bombardment raided Front Line Trenches. Two Coys were sent up to reinforce 15th Sherwoods in Front Line. Remainder manned the Reserve Line Trenches at Croix Barbee. | Report attached |
| Neuve Chapelle | 31-5-16 | 5 p.m | Relieved 15th Sherwood Foresters in Front Line Trench. | |
| | 1.6.16 | | One Coy of 2/8 Worcester Regt attached to the Battn for Instruction. | |
| | 2.6.16 | | Germans made a Bombing Demonstration against Centre Coy. Five bombs were thrown into our trench - no damage. Lieut H.C. Kinnel saved the lives of two men by throwing himself flat on a German Bomb which had been thrown into our trench. He was wearing a Steel Waistcoat at the time, and this save him from serious injury. For this he was awarded the M.C. | |
| | 3.6.16 | | Front Line Trenches. No Incident | |
| | 4.6.16 | | Ditto | |
| | 5.6.16 | | Ditto | |

A.T. Radclien Maj

Army Form C. 2118.

# WAR DIARY
## or
## INTELLIGENCE SUMMARY.
(Erase heading not required.)

Instructions regarding War Diaries and Intelligence Summaries are contained in F.S. Regs., Part II. and the Staff Manual respectively. Title pages will be prepared in manuscript.

| Place | Date | Hour | Summary of Events and Information | Remarks and references to Appendices |
|---|---|---|---|---|
| Neuve Chapelle | 6.6.16 | — | Front Line Trenches. No Incident. | |
| — | 7.6.16 | — | Ditto | |
| — | 8.6.16 | 9 p.m. | In Co-operation with Artillery, Trench Mortar and M.G. we made a Raid on the Enemy front Line. During this raid, we captured a German Machine Gun and killed, it is estimated 30 Germans. Lt Col Roberts and Capt H.A. Butt were killed and Lt H. Brown wounded. | Report attached |
| — | 9.6.16 | 3.30 p.m. | Battalion relieved by 15th Sherwoods | |
| Croix Barbee | 10.6.16 | — | Brigade reserve. Maj Vernon evacuated sick. | |
| — | 11.6.16 | — | Brigade Reserve. | |
| — | 12.6.16 | — | Ditto | |
| — | 13.6.16 | — | Ditto | |
| — | 14.6.16 | — | Ditto | |
| — | 15.6.16 | — | Batln relieved by 11th Royal Sussex Regt. Marched to Vielle Chapelle. | |
| Vielle Chapelle | 16.6.16 | — | Marched to Hingette. 35 Division in Corps Reserve. | |
| Hingette | 17.6.16 | — | In Billets. Corps Reserve. | |
| — | 18.6.16 | — | Ditto | |
| — | 19.6.16 | — | Ditto | |
| — | 20.6.16 | — | Ditto | |
| — | 21.6.16 | — | Ditto. Maj O.H. Packer takes over Command of the Bn from this date. | |

A.H. Packer

Army Form C. 2118.

# WAR DIARY
or
# INTELLIGENCE SUMMARY.
(Erase heading not required.)

Instructions regarding War Diaries and Intelligence Summaries are contained in F. S. Regs., Part II. and the Staff Manual respectively. Title pages will be prepared in manuscript.

| Place | Date | Hour | Summary of Events and Information | Remarks and references to Appendices |
|---|---|---|---|---|
| Hangette | 22.6.16 | | Corps Reserve - In Billets | |
| -,,- | 23.6.16 | | Ditto - 105th Bde inspected by G.O.C. 1st Army. | |
| -,,- | 24.6.16 | | G.H.Q. ~~Corps~~ Reserve. | |
| -,,- | 25.6.16 | | Ditto | |
| -,,- | 26.6.16 | | Ditto Capt W.P.S. Forrel joined the Battn & Takes over the duties of 2nd in Comd. | |
| -,,- | 27.6.16 | | Ditto | |
| -,,- | 28.6.16 | | Part of Transport moved by Road to LUCHEUX - 3rd Army Area. Battalion ordered to be prepared to move at two hours notice | |
| -,,- | 29.6.16 | | Still awaiting orders to move - In billets at Hangette. In connection with our Raid on 8-6-16. | |
| -,,- | 30.6.16 | | Ditto First Welcome awarded the M.C. 9413 Sgt J. Upson 8578 Sgt J. Rainbird and 20894 Pte Kirby awarded the Military Medal. | |

A.L.Cadiu
Major
Comdg 14 (S) Br Gloucester Regiment

## 14th.(Service) Battalion Gloucestershire Regiment.

Report on Operations against the Right SubSection
NEUVE CHAPELLE on the night of 30th./31st.May 1916.

At 8-30 p.m. a runner arrived from the Front Line with a verbal message saying "Send Reinforcements, the Germans have broken through"
He was too breathless to say any more at the time, but I found out that he had met 2 Officers near LANSDOWN POST who gave him the verbal message.  He does not know who the officers were.
I immediately warned the Right Reserve Battalion to 'Stand to Arms' and also the Details of the 15th.SHERWOODS, who had come out of the Front Line for the Relief.  They forthwith occupied their appointed positions.
I telephoned 105th.Brigade Head Quarters and sent 2nd.Lieutenant DEWDNEY there as laison officer.  I received orders from Brigade at 8-30 p.m. to send one Company to LANSDOWN POST and to hold the Reserve line with the remainder of the Battalion.
I had the 15th.SHERWOOD FORESTERS Machine Gunners and Battalion Head Quarters on the Right under Lieut.CRESSWELL and Lieut.WINCHERLEY, "Z"Company 14th.GLOUCESTERS next, then "X"Company and "W"Coy. on the left.
I despatched "Y"Company with the days rations, filled water bottles and ammunition under Lieut.H.C.KINRED to LANSDOWN POST where he arrived without incident at 9-35 p.m.  He reported to Colonel GORDON at once and placed himself under his orders.
I had two LEWIS guns of SHERWOODS in ST VAAST POST and two in emplacements in front of Reserve Battalion H.Q.  also two mobile guns, which I intended pushing forward in front of my line.  The whole under the command of Lieut.CRESSWELL.  All positions were taken up promptly and quietly and there was no confusion.  Everything worked perfectly in spite of the fact that all 2nd.in Command Companies and Coy.Sergeant Majors had gone up to the Front Line
No shells fell near the right of the Reserve line, but on the left near the SHRINE and the CROIX BARBEE Cross Roads, there was heavy shelling with shrapnel and H.E.
At 11-15 p.m I received word by runner from Col.GORDON, asking for half of "Y"Coy. which was in LANSDOWN POST to be sent up to Front Line.  This was immediately done and shortly afterwards the remainder of the Coy. was sent up,
At 11-30 p.m. I received order from Brogade Head Quarter to send another Company to LANSDOWN POST and "X"Coy. was immediately despatched fully equipped under Captain H.A.BUTT.  Orders were also received at the same time that the men in the Reserve Tranches could 'Stand Down' and the remainder of the Relief would take place on the night of the 31st.inst.  The two Coys. "W" and "Z" in under Captain WITTS and HANCOCK slept accoutred and ready to turn out at a moments.
In the course of the evening I received word from Offocers Commanding 17th. and 18th.LANCS FUS. saying they were standing by ready to support if required.  This support was not called for.
With further reference to hostile artillery fire:-
As near as could be judged from the Reserve Area the enemy commenced shelling our Front Line at 7-30 p.m.
At 8 p.m. they lengthened their range and fired on the Support Posts.
At 8-15 pm they again lengthened and fired on the Reserve Line at the SHRINE and CROIX BARBEE.
At 11-30 p.m. artillery fire ceased and with the exception of M.G.Fire the situation was normal.

(Sd)  G.C.Roberts,    Lt-Col.
Comdg.14th.(S) Battn.Gloucester Regt.

31-5-16.

**Full report of Raid on the night of 8th.June 1916.**

## Time Table of Events.

9 p.m. our artillery opened intense bombardment of enemy Front Line.
9-3 p.m. Hostile artillery retaliated on the whole of our Front Line with guns of every description.
9-5 p.m. Raiders and covering party left our Front Line and lay out in the middle of 'No Man's Land'.
Our T.Ms. commenced cutting operations on enemy wire.
9-20 p.m. artillery and T.Ms. lifted to enemy Support Trench and formed a barrage on point of attack.
9-25 p.m. raiders entered enemy trench.
Covering Party moved up to within 80 yards of enemy trench.
9-40 p.m. Raiders evacuated enemy trench.
10 p.m. Raiders returned to our lines.
10-20 p.m. Hostile artillery ceased.
10-30 p.m. Situation normal.

## Narrative.

At 9 p.m. our artillery opened an intense bombardment of enemy Front Line. Red rockets were sent up by the enemy almost immediately, and the enemy retaliated within 3 minutes.
Colonel ROBERTS, Commanding the Battalion was killed by the first shell that came over. Captain and Adjutant F.H.TOOP took over control of affairs and did excellant work in getting the raiders out under very trying circumstances, the 2nd. in Command Major VERNON being completely cut off by shell fire with the right Company of the line.
The Raiders went out for roughly 100 yards and lay down.
Actual raiders in front, the clearing up party 20 yards behind them.
AT 9-20 p.m. the artillery lifted and the raiders, followed by the clearing party followed. When within 20 yards of the enemy trench they were confronted by Machine Gun and Rifle fire.
They however, pushed forward and bombed their way into the line.
The first party to enter the trench was the left party under Captain BUTT, No sooner had they entered the trench than they were confronted by a party of Germans, the leader of whom was an Officer, this officer shot Captain BUTT, shattering his arm.
Pte.KIRBY immediately ran his bayonet through this Officer.
Pte.BULL who was with the party got Captain BUTT out of the trench and was bringing him back to our lines when he, Captain BUTT, was hit in the head and killed by a shell. Pte.BULL then sent for assistance, and remained with Captain BUTT until it arrived,
When Captain BUTT was hit Sergt.RAINBIRD who was with this party, took charge of them and continued the work of destruction. They bombed 3 dugouts and drove the Germans on to our artillery barrage in the rear where they were, either killed by shell or bombs.
This party then withdrew having been in the trench 20 minutes.
The right party entered the German trench led by 2nd.Lieut.MELDRUM, about 10 yards to the right they came on a Maxim Gun in an emplacement with the crew in readiness to fire. Pte.HOMER, who was with this party threw bombs at the crew. Pte.COHEN made a dash at them with the bayonet and despatched two of them the remainder made off but Pte.HOMER threw more bombs, and the whole of them were killed except one man, who was shot by 2nd.Lt.MELDRUM. The Machine Gun was very difficult to remove but was eventually got out and sent back to our lines. After sending the gun back, 2nd.Lt.MELDRUM with the rest of his party bombed dugouts in the vicinity, and then withdrew, having been in the line 20 minutes. The Centre Party under 2nd.Lt.BROWN were the last to enter. As they entered the trench, 2nd.Lt.BROWN, was hit by the back blast by one of our own bombs. Sergt.UPSON who was with this party took charge and after seeing 2nd.Lt.BROWN in a place of safety entered the enemy trench, and bombed their way up a C.T. This party destroyed a Machine Gun which was in position at point of entry. They remained in the trench for 15 minutes and then withdrew. Sergt.UPSON and Pte. SPEAKE were the last to leave the trench and they brought 2nd.Lt. BROWN back to safety under very heavy shell fire.

The Clearing Up Party under 2nd.Lieut.MENENDEZ , entered the German trench, but found little clearing up to do, owing to the through work done by the bombers.  After satisfying himself that all the bombers had withdrawn, and finding that nothing else could be done, 2nd.Lieut. MENENDEZ gave the order to withdraw, having been in the trench 20 minutes.  The whole of the raiders except 4 missing were back in our line at 10 p.m.  When 2nd.Lieut.MENENDEZ xxxxxxxxxxxxxxxxxxxxxxxxxx returned to our line he heard that Captain BUTT was still in 'No Man's Land' wounded.  He immediately volunteered to go out and find him. He found him in a shell hole about 80 yards from our line.  Finding him, as he thought dangerously wounded, and not wishing to rough handle him , he returned to our line and procured a stretcher.  He then returned and brought Captain BUTT back to our line under very heavy M.G.Fire.

Sgt.HOBSON (Battalion Signalling Sergeant) and Pte.FOWLER, laid a wire out from our front Line to the German line, with which he kept up constant communication with Battalion H.Q.  The work of Lt.R.N. AYLWARD and Lance Corporal of the R.Es. is also worthy of note. They entered the enemy trench after the raiders had left and demolished a Machine Gun emplacement.  They also rendered very valuable assistance in bringing back Pte.BERRYMAN who was very seriously wounded, under very heavy fire.  Sgt.TAYLOR was trying to bring Pte.BERRYMAN back, when the above Officer and N.C.O. gave assistance.  The work of our T.Ms. was very effective.  They cut the German wire most thoroughly , and also played havoc in the German Trenches.  I wish to conclude with a word of praise for the magnificent work done by our artillery, whose help made the raid the success it was.

Our casualties during the raid were:-

        Killed.    2 Officers        3 Other ranks.
        Wounded    1   "        15.  "   "
        Missing.                    4.

(Sd)    B.M.Vernon,
Major,
Comdg.14th.(S) Battn.Gloucester Regiment.

10-6-16.

105th Bde.
35th Div.

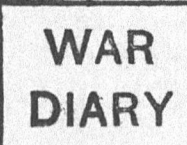

14th BATTALION

GLOUCESTERSHIRE REGIMENT.

1st to 31st JULY 1916

BS/
Army Form  July
14 Gloucesters
VOL 6

# WAR DIARY

## INTELLIGENCE SUMMARY.

(Erase heading not required.)

| Place | Date | Hour | Summary of Events and Information | Remarks and references to Appendices |
|---|---|---|---|---|
| HINGETTE | 1-7-16 | — | G.H.Q. Reserve. In Billets. Musketry, Physical Training – Bayonet fighting and Route Marching carried out. | |
| — | 2-7-16 | — | Ditto. Received orders to move by train to Bouquemaison on the 3rd inst to join 3rd Army. | |
| — | 3-7-16 | 4.15 a.m. | Marched to CHOQUES Station and entrained. | |
| LUCHEUX | — | 10 a.m. | Detrained at BOUQUE MAISON. Marched to Lucheux. In Billets. | |
| — | 4-7-16 | — | In Billets. | |
| — | 5-7-16 | — | Ditto – Short Route March. Musketry Training and Physical Training carried out. | |
| — | 6-7-16 | — | Route March and Tactical Exercise (Wood fighting) carried out. Received orders to march to Beauval on the 7th inst. | |
| Beauval | 7-7-16 | — | Marched to Beauval – In Billets. | |
| — | 8-7-16 | — | In Billets at Beauval – Musketry – Physical Training and Bayonet fighting carried out. | |
| — | 9-7-16 | — | Ditto. Received orders to march to Bus le ARTOIS. | |
| BUS | 10-7-16 | — | Marched to Bus le Artois. In Hutments. Received orders to march to WARLOY on the 11th inst. | |
| WARLOY | 11-7-16 | — | Marched to Warloy – In Billets. | |
| — | 12-7-16 | — | In Billets – 2nd in Command, Intelligence Officer and four Coy Commanders proceeded to front line by Motor Lorry to reconnoitre. | |
| — | 13-7-16 | — | Marched to Hilly. In Bivouac. W/H.Q.Ravine evacuated. | |
| Hilly | 14-7-16 | — | Marched to Bois les Celestines, where the Bn remained for four hours. | ↓ |
| Bois les Celestines | — | — | Marched to Grove Town. In Bivouac for one night. | 4 |
| Grove Town | 15-7-16 | — | Marched to Bellon Wood. | |

W P Nosely Major
Commdg 14th Bn Gloucester Regt

Army Form C. 2118.

# WAR DIARY
## or
## INTELLIGENCE SUMMARY.
(Erase heading not required.)

Instructions regarding War Diaries and Intelligence Summaries are contained in F.S. Regs., Part II. and the Staff Manual respectively. Title pages will be prepared in manuscript.

| Place | Date | Hour | Summary of Events and Information | Remarks and references to Appendices |
|---|---|---|---|---|
| Billon Wood | 16·7·16 | — | In Bivouac | |
| Maricourt | 17·7·16 | — | Relieved 2nd Suffolks in Support Trenches at Breguetoire | |
| — | 18·7·16 | — | In Support at Breguetoire. Shelled heavily. | |
| — | 19·7·16 | — | Relieved 16th Cheshires in Front Line in Trones Wood. Casualties Staff & Lewis killed – 4 officers wounded (23 men killed – 70 wounded – 10 missing). | |
| — | 20·7·16 | — | Batt relieved by 2nd Royal Scots. | |
| — | 21·7·16 | — | In Bivouacs at Talus Bois. | |
| — | 22·7·16 | — | Ditto – Warned to Stand by to Support 2nd Inf Bde | |
| — | 23·7·16 | — | In Bivouacs Near CARNOY | |
| — | 24·7·16 | 2:30 AM | In Reserve in CASEMENT TRENCH. Casualties Slight. Intermittent Shelling | |
| — | 25·7·16 | — | Ditto – Do – Reinforcements arrived from 56th I.B.D. – 200 other ranks. | |
| — | 26·7·16 | — | Relieved 19th Lancs Fus: BERNAFAY WOOD. – Shelled heavily. Working parties on Support trenches. | |
| — | 27·7·16 | — | In Support. BERNAFAY Trench. Working parties on Communication trenches — ditto — | |
| — | 28·7·16 | — | In Support – ditto – ditto – | |
| — | 29·7·16 | — | Ditto. Trench heavily bombarded for 1½ hours. | |
| | 30·7·16 | 10:30 PM | Relieved by 39th I.Bde Inf. Trench previous and during relief trench and roads heavily bombarded with H.E. and asphyxiating Gas Shells. Casualties slight. | |
| | 31·7·16 | — | In Bivouac near Carnoy | |
| | | 4 AM | Marched to Sand Pit Valley. | |

b P S Food
Major.
Commanding 14th Gloucester Rgt.

105th Brigade.
35th Division.

1/14th BATTALION

GLOUCESTERSHIRE REGIMENT

AUGUST 1916

Army Form C. 2118.

Vol 7

# WAR DIARY
or
# INTELLIGENCE SUMMARY.
(Erase heading not required.)

| Place | Date | Hour | Summary of Events and Information | Remarks and references to Appendices |
|---|---|---|---|---|
| SAND PIT VALLEY | 1.8.16 | 6.30 PM | Battalion marched to BOIS de TAILLES | |
| BOIS de TAILLES | 2.8.16 | | Training in Camp. | |
| Ditto | 3.8.16 | | Training in Camp | |
| Ditto | 4.8.16 | | Training in Camp. | |
| | 5.8.16 | 2 PM | Battalion marched to MERICOURT (5 MILES) and entrained | |
| | 6.8.16 | 2 AM | Battalion detrained at SALEUX and marched to RIENCOURT (13 Miles) | |
| RIENCOURT | 7.8.16 | | Battalion in billets | |
| | 8.8.16 | | Battalion training and re-fitting. | |
| | 9.8.16 | | Battalion training. Attacking and consolidating positions. Orders received to move | |
| | 10.8.16 | 6 AM 1.30 PM | Transport left by route march (Brigaded) via DAOURS to CITADEL. Battalion marched to HANGEST and entrained for MERICOURT | |
| | | 8.0 PM | Battalion detrained and marched to CITADEL XIII Corps area. | |
| CITADEL | 11.8.16 | | Battalion rested. | |
| | 12.8.16 | | Battalion training. Attack and Specialists training - Lewis Guns, Bombers, Signallers. | |
| | 13.8.16 | | Divine Service. Inspection by Div. G.O.C. | |
| | | 9 PM | Working Party 580 men. Digging trenches in vicinity of TRONES WOOD - MALTZ HORN Farm. | |
| | 14.8.16 | 6 AM | Working Party 3 Officers 200 men - Ditto - Ditto - 6 wounded Casualties NIL | |

# WAR DIARY or INTELLIGENCE SUMMARY

Army Form C. 2118

| Place | Date | Hour | Summary of Events and Information | Remarks and references to Appendices |
|---|---|---|---|---|
| CITADEL | 14.8.16 | 6.30 AM | Working party (8 Officers 500 O.R.) returned. | |
| | | 4.45 PM | Working party (3 " 200 ") " | |
| | | 5.0 PM to 6.0 | 1st Working party on Physical exercises and Arms drill. | |
| " | 15.8.16 | 8.30 AM | Battalion practised the Attack. Specialists carried out training. | |
| | 16.8.16 | 6.0 AM | Working party (8 Officers. 400 O.R.) | |
| | | 9.0 " | Remainder of Battalion carried out training | |
| | 17.8.16 | | Physical training and musketry drills | |
| | 18.8.16 | 9.0 " | Practised the Attack – Getting in and out of trenches quickly – Rapid wiring under R.E. Supervision. | |
| | 19.8.16 | | Rested | |
| | | 7.30 AM | Marched to LANCASTER & DAWSON Trenches and relieved 2nd Lincolns (24.2 Div.) | |
| Lancaster & Dawson Trenches | 20.8.16 | | Officers reconnoitred to front line. Cleaning and improving trenches | |
| | | 11.30 PM | Battalion left for front line trenches to A. | |
| LAMB Trench & overflow Trench (reserve) | 21.8.16 | 5.0 AM | The Battalion left trench to reconnoitre and if possible occupy a Strong point in enemy trenches. Relieving 16th Cheshire Regt. = 2 Corpls LAMB Trench. 2 O.R. wounded. 2 Corps Overflow Trench. | |
| | | 5.30 " | Party returned and reported point strongly held with Machine Guns. 2/Lt Mitchell and 4 O.R. wounded. | |
| | 22.8.16 | 4.30 AM | Enemy Artillery very active, constantly shelled 1st and 2nd lines. | |
| | | | A party of about 50 enemy left strong point and advanced towards our trenches, they were driven back by Lewis Gun fire. | |
| | | 5.0 " | A small party (about 10) of enemy left strong point and advanced, they were driven back by Lewis Gun and rifle fire. Repaired trenches. Casualties Officers 3 wounded O.R. 4 Killed #3 wounded | A.D.S.S./Forms/C. 2118. |

Army Form C. 2118.

# WAR DIARY
## or
## INTELLIGENCE SUMMARY.
(Erase heading not required.)

Instructions regarding War Diaries and Intelligence Summaries are contained in F. S. Regs., Part II. and the Staff Manual respectively. Title pages will be prepared in manuscript.

| Place | Date | Hour | Summary of Events and Information | Remarks and references to Appendices |
|---|---|---|---|---|
| LAMB Trench | 23.8.16 | | Our 8" How bombarded the enemys Strong point. | |
| | | 5.30 PM | Attack on Strong point prepared in conjunction with 13th Cheshires. | |
| | | | The attack was not carried out owing to insufficient damage being done to enemys trench. | |
| | | 7-7 PM | Enemy heavily bombarded our trenches 2nd line especially, also support lines, two craters blown on road. Casualties. O.R. 2 Killed - 34 Wounded - 9 missing. | |
| | | 11.30 PM | Battalion relieved by Leinster Regiment. Enemy bombarding Communication trenches. | |
| BRANTAY FARM | 24.8.16 | 3 AM | Battalion rested. | |
| | 25.8.16 | | " " | |
| | | | Parades and inspections under O.C Companies. | |
| SAND PIT VALLEY | 26.8.16 | | Battalion marched to SAND PIT VALLEY. | |
| | 27.8.16 | | Divine Service. Heavy rain. | |
| | | 9.30 | Parades under Company Commanders. | Beef |
| | 28.8.16 | | 1st Draft Parade for kit under the Adjutant. | |
| | | | Battalion marched to Bois des TAILLES Heavy rain | |
| Bois des TAILLES | 29.7.16 | 11 PM | Transport marched under Brigade arrangements to PROUVILLE via COISY. | Jacket |
| | | 12 MN | Battalion marched to HEILLY | |
| | 30.7.16 | 5 AM | Entrained for CANDAS. | 17 |
| | | 10.30 PM | Battalion detrained and marched to PROUVILLE | |
| PROUVILLE | | 1.45 PM | Battalion reached PROUVILLE | |
| | 31.8.16 | 9.6 AM | Battalion marched to CROUCHES and billeted. A.G. Army inspected Drafts received since 14th July 1916. | 5th Cheshires C⁰ 3 |

Vol 8

Army Form C. 2118.

# WAR DIARY
## or
## INTELLIGENCE SUMMARY
(Erase heading not required.)

1/4 Gloucesters

| Place | Date | Hour | Summary of Events and Information | Remarks and references to Appendices |
|---|---|---|---|---|
| CROUCHES | 1.9.16 | 8.45 AM | The Battalion marched to LUCHEUX. | |
| LUCHEUX | " | 9.45 " | The Battalion proceeded to AGNEZ-lez-DUISANS by Motor lorries | |
| AGNEZ lez DUISANS | " | 12.0 NOON | Arrived and billeted in AGNEZ-lez-DUISANS. | |
| Do | 2.9.16 | 9.0 AM | L. & O.C. Companies proceeded to ARRAS to prepare for reliefs. | |
| " | " | 5.15 PM | Battalion marched to ARRAS and relieved 7th Leicesters Regt. 1 Coy Foresters Nicoll's Redoubt. 1 " Bosky Edge & St NICHOLAS Village. GAS alert. H.Q. & 2 Coys in ARRAS | |
| ARRAS | 3.9.16 | | Battalion in Reserve. Enemy shelled ARRAS intermittently. Very wet up to NOON. Dull afternoon. | |
| " | 4.9.16 | | Do to Do | |
| " | 5.9.16 | | Battalion in Reserve. Enemy Shelled ARRAS intermittently. Improved trenches. | |
| " | 6.9.16 | | Battalion " Reserve. L. Cpl T.H.Turner and Pte J. L. Bowler awarded Military Medal by Corps Commander. | |
| " | 7.9.16 | 8.0 AM | Working parties in July and August trenches 1 OR Killed. Draft of 37 OR arrived. | |
| " | 8.9.16 | 8.0 AM | Working parties " " " " " 5 " " 2 OR wounded. Gas alert. | |
| " | 9.9.16 | 8.0 AM | Working parties " July " August trenches | |
| " | 10.9.16 | 8.0 AM | Working parties " July " August trenches. Gas alert. Off. draft of 17 OR arrived | |
| " | 11.9.16 | 8.0 AM | " " " " " " " | |
| " | 12.9.16 | | Working parties - July and August trenches. Carrying party. T.M.Bombs to Dwars | |
| " | 13.9.16 | | " " " " " " | |
| " | 14.9.16 | | Working parties - July and August trenches | |

Army Form C. 2118.

# WAR DIARY
## or
## ~~INTELLIGENCE SUMMARY.~~
*(Erase heading not required.)*

Army reel. S 3

| Places | Date | Hour | Summary of Events and Information | Remarks and references to Appendices |
|---|---|---|---|---|
| ARRAS | 15.9.16 | 5 PM. | "W and "Z" Companies relieved 2 Companies 15th Cheshires in Support line J 3 Sub-Sector. | |
| " | 16.9.16 | 9 AM. | H.Qrs "X" and "Y" relieved 15th Cheshires in front line J 3 Sub Sector. Relief completed - 11.45 AM. | |
| "J 3 Sub Sect" | 17.9.16 | | G.O.C. Div. presented ribbons to Officers and O.Rs who had been awarded medals. etc | |
| | | | Repairing trenches. A few rifle grenades from enemy - No Casualties. That all artillery barrage. 20" | |
| - do - | 18.9.16 | | Heavy rain which caused a good deal of damage to trenches. | |
| | | | Repairs to trenches. Enemy very quiet. - No Casualties - Test call Artillery barrage 20 Secs | |
| - do - | 19.9.16 | | Fine bright morning - Trenches in bad state owing to rain. Repairs to trenches. | |
| - do - | 20.9.16 | | Repairing front line trenches. | |
| - do - | 21.9.16 | | Cleaning and repairing front line trenches. Sniping post established in Bay 100/4. | |
| - do - | 22.9.16 | | Enemy active with T.M. and rifle grenades, a large number of grenades were "duds". | |
| | | 4.45 PM. | Gas alert. Repairs to trenches. | |
| - do - | 23.9.16 | 4. PM. | Enemy Arty & T.M.s active, very little damage done, no Casualties. | |
| | | | Repairs to trenches. | |
| ARRAS | 24.9.16 | 10. AM. | Battalion relieved by 15th Cheshire Regt. 1 Coy FORESTIER - NICHOLS Redoubt. | |
| | | | 1 " St NICHOLAS Village and BOSKY Redoubt. | |
| | | | 2 " Convent ARRAS | |
| | | | H.Q. ARRAS | |
| " | 25.9.16 | 8. AM. | Working parties. AUGUST and JULY Avenues. | |
| " | 26.9.16 | 8. AM. | Working parties. August and JULY Avenues. | |

Army Form C. 2118.

# WAR DIARY
## or
## INTELLIGENCE SUMMARY
(Erase heading not required.)

| Place | Date | Hour | Summary of Events and Information | Remarks and references to Appendices |
|---|---|---|---|---|
| ARRAS | 27.9.16 | 8 AM | Working parties. AUGUST and JULY AVENUE | |
| " | 28.9.16 | 7 AM | Battalion relieved 16th Sherwood Foresters in J2 Sub sector. 2 Coys Front line 1 Coy immediate Support line 1 " BRITANNIA WORKS H.Q. AUGUST AVENUE. | |
| | | 8 PM | Working party. AUGUST AVENUE. | |
| J2 Sub Sector | 29.9.16 | | Quiet day. T.M. retaliation by both sides. No Casualties | |
| — do — | 30.9.16 | | Trench Mortar activity. Working parties on Front line and Support Trenches. | |

**Army Form C. 2118.**

14 Block Ref — V
Vol 9

L.7

# WAR DIARY
## or
## INTELLIGENCE SUMMARY.
*(Erase heading not required.)*

Instructions regarding War Diaries and Intelligence Summaries are contained in F.S. Regs., Part II. and the Staff Manual respectively. Title pages will be prepared in manuscript.

| Place | Date | Hour | Summary of Events and Information | Remarks and references to Appendices |
|---|---|---|---|---|
| ARRAS Sub Sector T.2 | 1.10.16 | | Trench mortar activity on both sides. Repairing trenches. No casualties. | |
| | 2.10.16 | | Quiet day. Very wet. | |
| | 3.10.16 | | Very wet day. T.M. active. No casualties. | |
| | 4.10.16 | | Usual activity. 1 O.R. Wounded. | |
| | 5.10.16 | | T.M. active on both sides. 1 Casualty. | |
| | 6.10.16 | | Relieved by 15th Hussars. Leave to Officers 2 N.C.Os. Looking etc. Battalion out of trenches. Officer Received Cross in the morning. July Acquit. N.C.O's. Congratulations on good work received by C.O. from G.O.C. Brigade. | |
| | 7.10.16 | | | |
| | 8.10.16 | | All Battalion found Congratulations again received from G.O.C. Brigade. working Parties | |
| | 9.10.16 | | | |
| T.1 Subsector | 10.10.16 | | Relieved 15th Hussars complete by 10.0. A.M. T.1. Sub sector. Situation Quiet. Sentries Quiet. Our Lookup Shelter one day. 2 Casualties. | |
| | 11.10.16 | | T.M. active during afternoon & evening. Blue retaliated. A boy in Trench 86 Blown in | |
| | 12.10.16 | | Our Artillery & T.M. assisted by M.G. fire. Rifle Grenades. Stopped him line fire about 30 minutes. Little retaliation from him. Casualties. 1 killed. 12 wounded. | 25. Hos |
| | 13.10.16 | | Artillery T.M. on both sides more active than usual. very little damage done. Increased fiveness. | |

# WAR DIARY
## or
## INTELLIGENCE SUMMARY.
*(Erase heading not required.)*

Army Form C. 2118.

| Place | Date | Hour | Summary of Events and Information | Remarks and references to Appendices |
|---|---|---|---|---|
| ARRAS, J.1. Subsector | 15/10/16 | | Except for afternoon strafe, very quiet. Very heavy artillery fire in the distance on our left tonight. | |
| " | 16/10/16 | | Very quiet on the whole of the front. | |
| " | 17.10.16 | | Very quiet on the whole of the front. | |
| " | 18.10.16 | | Relieved by 16th Cheshire Regt completed by 10 A.M. 2 Coys ARRAS. 1 St NICHOLAS VILLAGE & BOSKY REDOUBT. 1 Coy FORESTIER - NICHOLS REDOUBTS | |
| ARRAS. | 19.10.16 | | Very wet and cold. Working parties cancelled owing to weather. | |
| | 20.10.16 | | W.Y.Z. Companies working on trenches in J. sector. | |
| | 21.10.16 | | - Do - - Do - Intermittent shelling of ARRAS by enemy. No casualties. | |
| | 22.10.16 | | Battalion relieved 15th Cheshire Regiment in J. 3 Subsector. Enemy T.M's active. Casualties O.Rs 1 Killed 3 Wounded. | |
| J.3 Sub Sector | 23.10.16 | | Our Stokes guns very active. Work on trenches. Wiring party. Gas Alert | |
| | 24.10.16 | | Very quiet day. Revetting and repairing trenches. Wiring party in front of Bays 97,98,99. Enemy T.M's very active during afternoon. Our Artillery and Stokes guns did Considerable damage to German trenches. | |
| | 25.10.16 | 8 P.M. | Enemy's trenches raided by 15th S. Fusrs. Our artillery and T.M's very active, very feeble reply by Germans. Casualties. 1 Officer killed 1 O.R. wounded. | |
| | 26.10.16 | | Very quiet day. Gas Alert off. | |
| | 27.10.16 | | Very wet. T.M activity on both sides. | (F. H.C.) |

Army Form C. 2118.

# WAR DIARY
## or
## INTELLIGENCE SUMMARY.

(Erase heading not required.)

Instructions regarding War Diaries and Intelligence Summaries are contained in F. S. Regs., Part II. and the Staff Manual respectively. Title pages will be prepared in manuscript.

| Place | Date | Hour | Summary of Events and Information | Remarks and references to Appendices |
|---|---|---|---|---|
| ARRAS J.3 Sub Sect | 28.10.16 | | T.M. on both sides very active. Work on trenches, repairing damage by T.M.s | |
| | | 8.30 pm | Combined Artillery and T.M.s bombarded German lines and communications. Suspected reliefs by enemy. | |
| | 29/10/16 | | Usual T.M. activity on both sides, otherwise quiet day. Work on trenches continued. Heavy rain. | 1. Coy Forselini Y Nicholls Redoubts 1 " St Nicholas Village and Bosky Redoubt 2 " Convent ARRAS. |
| | 30.10.16 | 11.15 AM | Relieved by 15th Cheshire Regiment. | |
| | | 5.0 PM | Reinforcements of 36 O.R.s arrived. | |
| | 31.10.16 | | Battalion found working parties under Brigade instructions. Heavy rain. | |

W.S. Ford
Lieut. Col.
Comdg. 14th (S) Bn. Gloster Regt. (W. of E.)

4th •Gloucesters• (Volume 10)

# WAR DIARY
or
## INTELLIGENCE SUMMARY.

Army Form C. 2118.

Vol 10

| Place | Date | Hour | Summary of Events and Information | Remarks and references to Appendices |
|---|---|---|---|---|
| ARRAS. | 1.11.16 | 8 AM. | Working parties under Brigade arrangements. 1 O.R. wounded. | |
| | 2.11.16 | 8 AM. | Working parties under Bde arrangements | |
| | | 11 AM. | " Cancelled owing to very Bad weather. | |
| | 3.11.16 | 6.30AM | Relieved 16th Sherwoods in J.2 Sub Sector. 2 Companies in front line | |
| J.2 Sub Sector | | | 1 Company immediate support | |
| | | | 1 " " Britannia Works. | |
| | | 9.45AM | Relief Completed. | |
| | | 3.30PM | Bombardment of Enemy's trenches by 6", 4.5", Stokes Mortars, & M. Guns. Slight retaliation by T.M.s and a few heavy shells. No Casualties. Work continued on Trenches assisted by R.E.s and N.F. (Pioneers). | |
| " | 4.11.16 | | Quiet morning. | |
| | | 2.30PM | Our Stokes Guns active, slight retaliation by Enemy H.T.M.s damage done to Communication trench behind CUTHBERT Crater. No Casualties | L. 8 |
| | | 6. PM. | Gas alert. | |
| | 5.11.16 | | Quiet day. High wind. Gas alert off. Rebuilding damaged trenches in front and Support lines. | |
| | 6.11.16 | 3. PM. | Combined firing by Artillery and Stokes Guns on Enemy trenches. 2 O.Rs wounded. Very wet day. Repairing Trenches. Enemy T.Ms very active. | |
| | 7.11.16 | 7.30AM | Very wet day. Repairing of damaged trenches. Both sides active with T.M.s | C.H |

Army Form C. 2118.

# WAR DIARY
## or
## INTELLIGENCE SUMMARY.
(Erase heading not required.)

Instructions regarding War Diaries and Intelligence Summaries are contained in F. S. Regs., Part II. and the Staff Manual respectively. Title pages will be prepared in manuscript.

| Place | Date | Hour | Summary of Events and Information | Remarks and references to Appendices |
|---|---|---|---|---|
| Tr. Sub Sector ARRAS | 8.11.16 | | Heavy rain causing considerable damage to trenches. Repairing damage to trenches. Caused by Rain and Enemy T.M.s | |
| | | 3 P.M. | Our T.M.s active. Enemy retaliated with Heavy T.M. | |
| | 9.11.16 | | Quiet day. Repairing front and support line trenches. | |
| | 10.11.16 | | Enemy artillery and T.M.s active. Aircraft activity. Trenches repaired | |
| | 11.11.16 10. A.M. | | Relieved by 15th Sherwood Foresters. | |
| | | | 1 Coy. Nichols and FORESTIER Redoubt. | |
| | | | 1 " St Nicholas Village - Booby Redoubt. | |
| | | | 2 " Convent ARRAS | |
| ARRAS | 12.11.16 | | Battalion rested. 1. O.R wounded. | |
| | 13.11.16 | | Working parties under Brigade arrangements. Letter received from G.O.C. Congratulating all ranks on good work done during 13-14.6. | |
| | 14.11.16 | | — do — | |
| Tr. 1 Sub Sec | 15.11.16 10 A.M | | — do — | |
| | | | Relieved 16th Cheshire Regiment. 3 Companies in Front line | |
| | | A.M | 1 Company " Support " | |
| | | 11.12 | Casualties O.R.s 1 Killed 3 wounded. | |
| | | | 12" How. bombarded Enemy T.M. Emplacement; results very satisfactory. | |
| | 16.11.16 | 4 P.M. | Repairing front and support trenches. | |
| | | | Gas alert. | |
| | 17.11.16 | | Enemy Aircraft active. Sand bagging and revetting. Making new fire step in Support line. | |

355 Wt. W5141/1434 700,000 5/15 D.D. & L. A.D.S.S./Forms/C. 2118.

C.H

Army Form C. 2118.

# WAR DIARY
## or
## INTELLIGENCE SUMMARY.
*(Erase heading not required.)*

Instructions regarding War Diaries and Intelligence Summaries are contained in F.S. Regs., Part II. and the Staff Manual respectively. Title pages will be prepared in manuscript.

| Place | Date | Hour | Summary of Events and Information | Remarks and references to Appendices |
|---|---|---|---|---|
| J.1. Sub Sect. | 18.11.16 | | Aircraft activity. Our T.M⁵ and Artillery very active. Enemy retaliated with heavy T.M⁵. Very little damage done. Reconstructing Support line. Wiring in front of SAP 84. | |
| | 19.11.16 | | Very wet day. Cleaning trenches which had fallen in owing to rain. 3 O.R⁵ wounded. Gas sent off. Enemy retaliated with heavy T.M⁵ after our afternoon artillery straf⁵. Repairing trenches in front and support lines. | |
| | 20.11.16 | | | |
| | 21.11.16 | | Enemy very active with T.M⁵ did a lot of damage to our front line & Sap 5 and Sebastopol Avenue. | |
| | 22.11.16 | 11 P.M. | Repairing trenches in front and support lines. Enemy Aeroplane brought down in J" wiring in front of Saps 84, 87, 88. Shot by our machines. | |
| Arras. | 23.11.16 | | Throughout the day the enemy showed unusual activity with T.M⁵ and rifle grenades. No Casualties. Relieved by 16ᵗʰ Cheshire Regiment. | |
| | 24.11.16 | 2. P.M. | Carrying parties. A few small working parties, otherwise Battalion rested. | |
| | 25.11.16 | A.M. | Very wet day. Working parties under Brigade arrangements. | |
| | | 10. A.M. | All working parties cancelled. | |
| | 26.11.16 | 3. A.M. | Centre Battalion sent up S.O.S. signal. Battalion acted in accordance with Defence Scheme. | |
| | | 8. A.M. | Working parties under Brigade arrangements. Quiet day. | |
| J.2 Sub Sect. | 27.11.16 | 8. A.M. | Relieved 15ᵗʰ Sherwoods in J 2 Sub Sector. 2 Companies Front Line 1 Company Immediate Support 1 Company in Reserve | |
| | | | Quiet day. Work on trenches, repairing damage. | |

#353 Wt. W2544/1454 700,000 5/15 D. D. & L. A.D.S.S./Forms/C. 2118.

Army Form C. 2118.

# WAR DIARY
## INTELLIGENCE SUMMARY.
*(Erase heading not required.)*

| Place | Date | Hour | Summary of Events and Information | Remarks and references to Appendices |
|---|---|---|---|---|
| T.11 Sub-Sect | 28/11/16 | | Repairing front and support trenches. Enemy fired torpedoes and Rifle Grenades along the whole front during the day and night. 2 O.R'S wounded. | |
| | 29.11.16 | 2 P.M. | Quiet morning. Repairing front and support lines. T.M. activity on both sides. | |
| | 30.11.16 | 2.30 P.M. | Repairing front and Support lines. Our artillery and T.M'S bombarded enemy's lines, enemy retaliation very weak. | |
| | | 12. Non. | Gas Alert. Very Quiet night. | |

C Hancock Major

for. Comdg. 14th (S) Bn. Gloster Regt. (W. of E.)

# WAR DIARY
## INTELLIGENCE SUMMARY.
*(Erase heading not required.)*

Army Form C. 2118.

| Place | Date | Hour | Summary of Events and Information | Remarks and references to Appendices |
|---|---|---|---|---|
| In Sub Sect | 28/11/16 | | Repairing front and Support trenches. Enemy fired torpedoes and Rifle Grenades along the whole front during the day and night. 2 O.Rs Wounded. | |
| | 29/11/16 | | Quiet morning. Repairing front and support lines. | |
| | | 2. P.M. | T.M. activity on both sides. | |
| | 30/11/16 | | Repairing front and support lines | |
| | | 2.30 P.M | Our Artillery and T.Ms bombarded Enemy's lines, Enemy retaliation very weak. | |
| | | 12. Mdn. | Gas alert. Very Quiet night. | |

C Hancock Maj/x
for Comdg. 14th (S) Bn. Gloster Regt. (W. of E.)

# WAR DIARY or INTELLIGENCE SUMMARY

Army Form C. 2118.

14 Gloucester Regt
14th (Service) Bn.
Vol XI

| Place | Date | Hour | Summary of Events and Information | Remarks and references to Appendices |
|---|---|---|---|---|
| ARRAS J.2 Sub Sector | 1.12.16 | | Enemy retaliated, after our "Strafe", with T.Ms H.E. & Shrapnel, very little damage done. Work carried on in front and support lines, and wiring during the night. | |
| | 2.12.16 | | Repairing front and support lines. Quiet day. Advance parts from 2nd S.A.Inf arrived. Casualties 3 O.Rs wounded | |
| | 3.12.16 | 6 PM | Quiet day. Gas alert off. Relief commenced by 2nd S. African Infantry | |
| | | 10 " | Relief complete. | |
| DUISSANS | 4.12.16 | 10.45 AM | Companies marched independently to DUISSANS and billeted for the night. Battalion left by road and marched to MANIN and GIVENCHY LE NOBLE. | |
| | | 12.30 PM | Inspected by Divisional General. | |
| MANIN – GIVENCHY LE NOBLE | | 3.30 PM | Arrived new billets. 2 Coys MANIN. 2 Coys GIVENCHY. | |
| | 5.12.16 | | Battalion rested. Kit inspection. Cleaning billets. | |
| | 6.12.16 | 8 A.M. | Physical training and musketry. Cleaning billets. | |
| | 7.12.16 | | — Do — — Do — Cleaning billets | |
| | 8.12.16 | | — Do — — Do — | |
| | 9.12.16 | | — Do — — Do — Cleaning billets, making field ovens, constructing Rifle Range. | J.9 |
| | 10.12.16 | | — Do — — Do — | |
| | 11.12.16 | | Inspection by the A.D.M.S. 110 men marked for Base duties. Battalion paraded for inspection by G.O.C. 105 Bde. | CM |

# WAR DIARY
## or
## INTELLIGENCE SUMMARY.
(Erase heading not required.)

Army Form C. 2118.

| Place | Date | Hour | Summary of Events and Information | Remarks and references to Appendices |
|---|---|---|---|---|
| MANIN.— | 12.12.16 | | Companies under Company Commanders. Bayonet fighting, musketry. | |
| GIVENCHY LES- NOBLE | 13.12.16 | | Battalion paraded for inspection by G.O.C. 35th DIV. | |
| | 14.12.16 | | All companies Bayonet fighting under a Staff instructor | |
| | 15.12.16 | | men <s>were</s> inspected by A.D.M.S. on the 10th 1 not seen 34 men marked Bave. | |
| | 16.12.16 | | 2 Companies bathing at IZEL. 2 " training under the Commanders | |
| | | 5.30 P.M. | Lecture on Bayonet fighting by the Export. | |
| | 17.12.16 | | 2 Companies bathing at IZEL. Bayonet fighting under the Export | |
| | 18.12.16 | 10.15 A.M | Inspection by Corps Commander. Companies Training under Commanders | |
| | 19.12.16 | 8.0 A.M. | Musketry and Bayonet fighting | |
| | 20.12.16 | 5.30 A.M. | Musketry and Company training. Inspection by Corps Commander. | |
| | 21.12.16 | | Lecture on Bayonet fighting. 2 Companies talks. 2 Companies training under Commanders | |
| | 22.12.16 | | Training under Company Commanders. | |
| | 23.12.16 | | Musketry, Bombing and Sniping instruction carried out. | |

Army Form C. 2118.

# WAR DIARY
## or
## INTELLIGENCE SUMMARY.
(Erase heading not required.)

| Place | Date | Hour | Summary of Events and Information | Remarks and references to Appendices |
|---|---|---|---|---|
| MANIN - | 24/12/16 | | Companies training under Company Commanders. Specialists training. Voluntary Church. | |
| GIVECHY LE MOBLE | | | | |
| | 25.12.16 | | Church parade. Holiday | |
| | 26.12.16 | | Brigade Rifle competitions at AMBRINES. Inspection of men rejected by Corps Comdr, A.D.M.S. and C.O. by 3rd Army Commander. | |
| | 27.12.16 | | Brigade Rifle competition, falling plate won by "X" Coy. "Y" won Brigade 5'aside football. | |
| | 28.12.16 | 11. A.M. | Battalion left by route march for ARRAS via NOYELLE. VION and HABARCQ. | |
| | | 6.30 P.M. | Battalion billeted in ARRAS and attached to 9th Division. | |
| ARRAS | 29.12.16 | | Rested. Company Commanders reconnitred work for 30th | |
| | 30.12.16 | | Working parties in 8 hour reliefs of 100 men under R.E. constructing dug-out in I sector. Training of Specialists. | |
| | 31.12.16 | | Working parties as for 30th | |

C Hancock
Lieut. Col.
Comdg. 14th (S) Bn. Gloster Regt. (W.of E.)

Army Form C. 2118.

# WAR DIARY
## or
## INTELLIGENCE SUMMARY.
(Erase heading not required.)

| Place | Date | Hour | Summary of Events and Information | Remarks and references to Appendices |
|---|---|---|---|---|
| ARRAS | 1.1.17 | 8. AM | Working parties in Support and Reserve lines under the orders of 9th Division | |
| | | 10." | Working cancelled owing to Operations. | |
| | | 5.30" | 12½ N.C.O's + men left for 55" I.B. Depôt rejected unfit by A.D.M.S. | |
| | 2.1.17 | 8. AM | 3 Shifts of 100 men each working in Reserve line, constructing "Dug Outs" | |
| | | 4. PM | Specialist training carried out | |
| | | 12. M.N. | | |
| | 3.1.17 | 8. AM | Working parties as on previous day. | |
| | | | Specialist training carried out. Lecture by Medical Officer. | |
| | 4.1.17 | 8. AM | — do — | |
| | | 10.45 PM | Enemy bombarded ARRAS with Gas shells. No Casualties. | |
| | 5.1.17 | 8. AM | Working parties under the orders of 9th Division. | |
| | | | Specialist training carried out. Lecture by Medical Officer. | |
| | | 10. PM | Enemy bombarded ARRAS with Gas shells. 1 O.R. gassed. | |
| | 6.1.17 | | 1st and 2nd shifts of working parties cancelled. | |
| | | 10. AM to 4. PM | Heavy bombardment of Enemy's lines in front of I Sector by our Artillery. No retaliation on ARRAS. | L.10 |
| | 7.1.17 | 8. AM | Working parties under orders of 9th Div. Specialist training. | |
| | 8.1.17 | " | — do — | |
| | 9.1.17 | | — do — | |

Edward Cartwright Lieut. Col.
Comdg. 14th (S) Bn. Gloster Regt. (W. of E.)

Army Form C. 2118.

# WAR DIARY
## or
## INTELLIGENCE SUMMARY.
(Erase heading not required.)

| Place | Date | Hour | Summary of Events and Information | Remarks and references to Appendices |
|---|---|---|---|---|
| ARRAS | 10/1/19 to 20/1/19 inclusive | | Working Parties under orders of 9th Division. Continuous work. 3 Parties Daily each working 8 hours. Nature of work Dugouts. | |
| | 22/1/19 to 31/1/19 | | Working Parties under orders 17th Corps Signals. Nature of work, digging trenches for cables, and fitting in for cables & fixing in. | |
| | 1/2/19 | | Battery Hdqrs moved from Arras to Montenescourt | |

A. W. Wras Capt adj

Comdg 468(S) Bn Cheshire Regt. (M E.F)

Army Form C. 2118.

14 Gloucester Rgt

Vol/3

# WAR DIARY
## or
## INTELLIGENCE SUMMARY.
*(Erase heading not required.)*

Instructions regarding War Diaries and Intelligence Summaries are contained in F. S. Regs., Part II. and the Staff Manual respectively. Title pages will be prepared in manuscript.

| Place | Date | Hour | Summary of Events and Information | Remarks and references to Appendices |
|---|---|---|---|---|
| ARRAS | 1/2/17 | | Working Parties under 17th Corps Signals. Nature of work, digging trenches for cables, and fixing in. Battalion Headquarters moved from Arras to Moncheaux. Draft 395 O.R. joined from Brigade Hqrs. Bonville. (Normal size men) | |
| | 2/2/17 | | Battalion marched out of Arras 5.0 A.M. to Ruthe St Quintin, and billeted there for the night. | |
| | 3/2/17 | | Battalion marched out of Ruthe St Quintin at 1.30. P.M. Draft of 80. O.R. (Normal size men) joined from Divisional Training Depot Battalion. Battalion accompanying and training | |
| MONCHEAUX | 4/2/17 | | Training under Company arrangements. | |
| | 5/2/17 | | do | |
| | 6/2/17 | | do - 2931 Men rejected and to Base | |
| | 7/2/17 | | Battalion marched out of Moncheaux and Billeted at 2 Companies at Newviccete at Beauvoir. 2 Companies 2 Hqrs. at Newviccete | |
| | 8/2/17 to 18/2/17 | | Battalion marched to Gezaincourt and Billeted for 1 night. Battalion marched to Fessells and remained there under the 18 of Febry. 1917. Training under Company arrangements. Specialists under Specialists Officers | |
| | 19/2/17 | | Battalion marched to Wiencourt, Billeted there 2 nights | |

Army Form C. 2118.

# WAR DIARY
## INTELLIGENCE SUMMARY
*(Erase heading not required.)*

Instructions regarding War Diaries and Intelligence Summaries are contained in F. S. Regs., Part II. and the Staff Manual respectively. Title pages will be prepared in manuscript.

| Place | Date | Hour | Summary of Events and Information | Remarks and references to Appendices |
|---|---|---|---|---|
| CHILLY | 20/2/17 | | Battalion marched to Yzely. Billeted there 1 night. | |
| " | 21/2/17 | | Battalion took over trenches from the French, in the Cois sector. | |
| " | 22/2/17 | | Relief complete in the early hours of the morning. Trenches in a very bad condition, in must case much and water well above the knee. | |
| " | 23/2/17 | | Trenches very bad, cleaning & draining where possible. Then very quiet, at 7.30. p.m. the whole of the Units front was heavily bombarded, this lasted until 8.45. p.m. French & our Artillery replied vigorously. Casualties:- 2. Killed 2. Wounded | |
| " | 24/2/17 | | Trenches very bad. Sharp bombardment during afternoon, increasing towards evening. Large number of Aerial Torpedoes fired on front line. Casualties 1. Killed 12. WOUNDED. | |
| " | 25/2/17 | | Same as previous day. Casualties. 1 Killed. 1 wounded. 1 Officer 2nd/Lt N. P. Hayward wounded. | |
| " | 26/2/17 | | Enemy raided dug outs in front line. P.P. Triangle, but was driven off. Same dawn. Enemy fairly active, during the whole of the day. Casualties 3. Killed Casualties. Nil. 2. Wounded | |
| " | 27/2/17 | | Very quiet, except for M.G. fire, which increased during hours of darkness. Casualties. Nil. | |
| " | 28/2/17 | | Very quiet, except for snipers, who were very active. Condition of trenches still very bad. Casualties. Nil. | |

W.S.S. Ford
Lieut. Col.
Comdg. 14th (S) Bn. Gloster Regt. (W. of E.)

Army Form C. 2118.

14th Gloster Regt.

Vol 14

L.12

# WAR DIARY
# ~~INTELLIGENCE SUMMARY.~~
*(Erase heading not required.)*

| Place | Date | Hour | Summary of Events and Information | Remarks and references to Appendices |
|---|---|---|---|---|
| C HILL J Sector | 1/3/17 | | Relieved in the Trenches by the 15th Sherwoods. Relief complete by 10.30 p.m. Battalion proceeded to Rougeuts & Maucourt, Hqrs. P.C. LE MANS. Duty Supporting Battalion. | |
| " | 2/3/17 | | Battalion in Rougeuts & Maucourt. Duty Supporting Battalion. All Ranks resting and cleaning up. | |
| " | 3/3/17 | | Battalion in Rougeuts & Maucourt. 150 O.R. Cleaning & clearing communication Trenches. Ration Carrying Party for left Company 15th Sherwoods. 1 Officer. 50. O.R. carrying party. R.E. material to front line. | |
| " | 4/3/17 | | Battalion in Rougeuts & Maucourt. 200. O.R. Cleaning & clearing communication Trenches. Ration carrying party for left Company 15th Sherwoods. | |
| " | 5/3/17 | | Battalion in Rougeuts at Maucourt. Work same as 4th inst. | |
| " | 6/3/17 | | do. do. do. | |
| " | 7/3/17 | | Relieved by 20 th Lancashire Fusiliers. Battalion out of Rougeuts five nights. Battalion marched out of Rougeuts in the morning and arrived at Camp Klacainille 12 NOON. D.24. a. 5. 9. | |

Army Form C. 2118.

# WAR DIARY
## or
## INTELLIGENCE SUMMARY.
(Erase heading not required.)

| Place | Date | Hour | Summary of Events and Information | Remarks and references to Appendices |
|---|---|---|---|---|
| DECAUVILLE | 8/3/17 | | Camp Decauville. All Ranks resting and Cleaning. | |
| | 9/3/17 | | Camp Decauville. Training, all Companies, under Company arrangement. | |
| | 10/3/17 | | do . do do | |
| | 11/3/17 | | do . do do | |
| | 12/3/17 | | do do do | |
| | 13/3/17 | | do do do. | |
| | 14/3/17 | | Camp Decauville. Battalion in the attack. Company training. Batt. moved to Rainies in the morning where it rested preparatory to going into the trenches. | |
| LIHONS | 15/3/17 | | The battalion relieved the 20th D.L.I. in the LIHONS sector. The Y.W.x. Companies were out being supplied by 2.30 P.M. 15-3-17. Quiet. Trenches were in the front line. The rest of the day was Quiet. Trenches were cleaned amp; anti-cleaned. Casualties. NIL | |
| | 16/3/17 | | Energetic patrols were sent out from each company to ascertain whether enemy front line was held. All patrols reported him to be | |

# WAR DIARY or INTELLIGENCE SUMMARY

Army Form C. 2118.

| Place | Date | Hour | Summary of Events and Information | Remarks and references to Appendices |
|---|---|---|---|---|
| LIHONS | 17/3/17 | | At 7.30 AM our night coy put up a smoke barrage to screen the huts in our right to avoid the enemy. At 5.30 pm our advance patrol who reported the enemy front line again pushed out. They took the enemy front line and patrols were again pushed out. Casualties Nil. | |
| | 18/3/17 | | We had moved forward to patrols in "Blackenny" trench. Patrols were again pushed out; there were relieved by the 15th Staffordshire Regmt. our batt. was being in support as reserve. | |
| | 19/3/17 | | Battalion returned to LIHONS where work on roads was commenced. | |
| | 20/3/17 | | Working parties at — full two strings on roads at LIHONS | |
| | 21/3/17 | | do | do |
| | 22/3/17 | | do | do |
| | 23/3/17 | | Battalion moved to CHAULNES after work on railway at Chaulnes station. | |

Army Form C. 2118.

# WAR DIARY
## or
## INTELLIGENCE SUMMARY.
(Erase heading not required.)

Instructions regarding War Diaries and Intelligence Summaries are contained in F. S. Regs., Part II and the Staff Manual respectively. Title pages will be prepared in manuscript.

| Place | Date | Hour | Summary of Events and Information | Remarks and references to Appendices |
|---|---|---|---|---|
| CURCHY | 24/3/17 | | Batt. working at full strength on railway between Chaulnes and Necle | |
| " | 25/3/17 | | Work on Chaulnes - Necle railway continued. Instruction firing rifle grenades with Batt. Bombing Officer where possible | |
| " | 26/3/17 | | do. do. | |
| " | 27/3/17 | | do. do. | |
| " | 28/3/17 | | Work on Chaulnes - Necle - Necle railway continued. Demonstration to Batt. of S.O.S. signal. | |
| " | 29/3/17 | | Work on Chaulnes - Necle railway continued. | |
| " | 30/3/17 | | Working parties at full Batt. strength working on railway round Necle station | |
| " | 31/3/17 | | Do | |

W. F. S. Ford
Lieut. Col.
Comdg. 14th (S) Bn. Gloster Regt. (W. of E.)

1-4-17

14th GLOSTER REGT

Vol 15

# WAR DIARY
## or
## INTELLIGENCE SUMMARY.

Army Form C. 2118.

(Erase heading not required.)

| Place | Date | Hour | Summary of Events and Information | Remarks and references to Appendices |
|---|---|---|---|---|
| HOMBLEUX | 1/4/17 | | The Battalion moved from CURCHY to work on NESLE-HAM-railway line. Work filling craters. On completion of work the battalion went into new huts at HOMBLEUX. | |
| " | 2/4/17 | | Battalion at work on railway East of K.P. 53. | |
| " | 3/4/17 | | Battalion working on roads NESLE-HAM-railway. | |
| " | 4/4/17 | | do do | |
| " | 5/4/17 | | Companies at disposal of O.C. Coys in the morning. In the afternoon attack in open Warfare war formation by the battalion. | |
| " | 6/4/17 | | Work on railway line EAST of K.P. 52. | |
| " | 7/4/17 | | Working parties at HOMBLEUX Station. | |
| " | 8/4/17 | | Training by companies in attack Musketry etc. | |
| " | 9/4/17 | | Companies at disposal of O.C. Companies in the morning, & the afternoon the battalion practised the attack in open Warfare. | L. 13 |
| " | 10/4/17 | | do do | |

W.S. Forster Lieut. Col.
Comdg. 14th (S) Bn Gloster R.

Army Form C. 2118.

# WAR DIARY
## or
## INTELLIGENCE SUMMARY.
*(Erase heading not required.)*

Instructions regarding War Diaries and Intelligence Summaries are contained in F. S. Regs., Part II. and the Staff Manual respectively. Title pages will be prepared in manuscript.

| Place | Date | Hour | Summary of Events and Information | Remarks and references to Appendices |
|---|---|---|---|---|
| HOMBLEUX | 10/4/17 | | The Batt practiced the attack in open Warfare. | |
| MONCHY-LAGACHE | 12/4/17 | | The Batt moved to MONCHY LAGACHE in Divisional Reserve. In the morning Coy were at disposal of Coy officer. Specialists were training with the specialist officer. In the afternoon specialists continued their training in the rest of the Batt worked on the MONTICOURT - TREFCON — | |
| " | 13/4/17 | | do do do | |
| " | 14/4/17 | | do do do | |
| " | 15/4/17 | | do do do | |
| GRICOURT | 16/4/17 | | The Batt relieved the 18th Lancashire Fusiliers in the outpost line in front of GRICOURT. There coys were in the outpost in Coy in support in FRESNOY. The relief was completed without incident. | |
| " | 17/4/17 | | The day of the 17th was exceptionally quiet. Our aircraft were very active, the enemy has yet discovered our outpost line. Several patrols went out but is now withdrawn on our line. Knuck with the enemy. | Lieut. Col. [signature] Comdg. 14th (S) Bn. Gloster Regt. |

8353 Wt. W2544/1454 700,000 5/15 D. D. & L. A.D.S.S./Forms/C. 2118.

# WAR DIARY or INTELLIGENCE SUMMARY.

Army Form C. 2118.

Comdg. 14th (S) Bn. Gloster Regt. (W. of E.)
Lieut. Col. E.J. [signature] C.O.

| Place | Date | Hour | Summary of Events and Information | Remarks and references to Appendices |
|---|---|---|---|---|
| GRICOURT | 18/4/17 | | We were heavily shelled in day and night in considerable numbers. It is very probable the enemy has not yet discovered our exact posts. Patrols were sent out and reported all places visited to be unoccupied by the enemy. | |
| " | 19/4/17 | | The enemy were again seen shelling CRICOURT and TROIS SAUVAGE also a small copse at M.17.C central. As neither of the last two places are not occupied by our garrison we have not yet been surprised by Aeroplane planes to the fact that he knew not yet been able to observe our position. Enemy artillery was so active to-day. At 2.10 p.m. an enemy plane flew over our own trenches at a very low altitude. It was fired on by our Lewis gun at Brendon gun without effect. The enemy also had received balloon up at great height. | |
| " | 20/4/17 | | Enemy artillery again active. FRESNOY was shelled heavily also Bn. H.Q. We dispersed an enemy working party with our artillery fire. At night we were relieved by the 15th Cheshire Regt., the relief was complete by 11 p.m. and was carried out without casualties. | |

Army Form C. 2118.

# WAR DIARY
## or
## INTELLIGENCE SUMMARY.
(Erase heading not required.)

Comdg. 14th (S) Bn. Gloster Regt. (W. of E.)
Lieut. Col. ................................
E. J. Peel

| Place | Date | Hour | Summary of Events and Information | Remarks and references to Appendices |
|---|---|---|---|---|
| KEEPERS LODGE | 22/4/17 | | Battalion Working Parties at full strength in the BROWN LINE. | |
| " | 23/4/17 | | do. do. do. | |
| " | 24/4/17 | | do. do. do. 2 men killed | |
| GRICOURT | 25/4/17 | | on the ST QUENTIN Rd near BOIS DE MOLON. The Battalion relieved the 10th Shropshire Yorks in the GRICOURT sector. The relief was completed without incident. There was considerable shelling during the night. | |
| " | 26/4/17 | | The last 24 hours have been very quiet. Enemy flying low. Planes over the German lines by our planes. | |
| " | 27/4/17 | | Things have been much more lively during the last 24 hours. Heavy shelling in the region of our Hd. Qrs. by his batteries. General activity by both sides. Planes occupied MONIDIER. 6 party of 2 officers and 20 O.R's. From 4 a.m. to 5.10 a.m. They regained our line without Casualties — activity a lot. Raid again contacted. The Lewins retaliated to our Bollegs turn in GRICOURT and throughly | |
| | 28/4/17 | | | |

**Army Form C. 2118.**

# WAR DIARY
## or
## INTELLIGENCE SUMMARY.
*(Erase heading not required.)*

Instructions regarding War Diaries and Intelligence Summaries are contained in F. S. Regs., Part II. and the Staff Manual respectively. Title pages will be prepared in manuscript.

| Place | Date | Hour | Summary of Events and Information | Remarks and references to Appendices |
|---|---|---|---|---|
| GRICOURT | 28/4/17 | M 20. a & b. | Shelling of GRICOURT not as heavy as usual. Several enemy planes flew over our lines during the day then our planes were brought into but without effect. | |
| | 29/4/17 | | The battalion was relieved by the 1/4th West Yorkshire Regiment. The relief was carried out quietly one experiencing. Before the relief the enemy attempted to work on our advance posts on our own side. It is thought with casualties. On Counties were seen were killed being relieved the battalion marched by platoons to VILLEVEQUE. | |
| | 30/4/17 | | | |

W. F. Stood, Lieut. Col.
Comdg. 14th (S) Bn. Gloster Regt. (W. of E.)

**Army Form C. 2118.**

# WAR DIARY or INTELLIGENCE SUMMARY.

*(Erase heading not required.)*

14th Gloster

Vol 16

| Place | Date | Hour | Summary of Events and Information | Remarks and references to Appendices |
|---|---|---|---|---|
| VILLEVEQUE | 1/5/17 | | First day in Divisional Reserve was spent in refitting and general cleaning up. | |
| | 2/5/17 | | Companies at the disposal of their O.C.s for training firing took place by all companies from Lee Enfield. Working parties at Crater West of Pouilly, Rantville, Willedrake Road. The battalion attended the bath at TERTRY by companies. | |
| | 3/5/17 | | Training of specialists by specialists officers. Companies at disposal of their O.C.s for training. Snipers firing in course of open manage. | |
| | 4/5/17 | | Battalion practised the attack in open Warfare. Snipers fired long range. | |
| | 5/5/17 | | Companies at disposal of their O.C.s for training. Specialists training of specialists. | |
| | 6/5/17 | | Do. Do. | |
| | 7/5/17 | | Do. Do. | |
| | 8/5/17 | | During day preparation for duty in the front line. Right Support line. The relief was carried out without incident. | L.F. |

Army Form C. 2118.

# WAR DIARY
or
# INTELLIGENCE SUMMARY.
(Erase heading not required.)

| Place | Date | Hour | Summary of Events and Information | Remarks and references to Appendices |
|---|---|---|---|---|
| KEEPERS LODGE. | 9/5/17 | | We had very little hostile shelling. Our guns were pretty active. Companies worked on BROWN LINE. | |
| " | 10/5/17 | | Fairly quiet day. Our guns harassed the enemy 1500 m. our planes flew over in order to destroy every kite balloon but the balloon was lowered before our planes could reach them. The hostile worked on Outpost in front of GRICOURT. Great hostile artillery and aerial activity during day. Enemy planes forced to retire by our planes not ours. Enemy aircraft guns. Companies at work on Outpost line. | |
| | 11/5/17 | | Very little aerial or artillery activity during day. Enemy artillery active during the night. Companies working on Outpost line. | |
| | 12/5/17 | | Passing the day out quiet, enemy's everything was exceptionally quiet. We relieved the Sherwood Foresters in the GRICOURT Sector. The relief was carried out without incident. The whole of our front was patrolled during the night. | |

Army Form C. 2118.

# WAR DIARY
## or
## INTELLIGENCE SUMMARY.
*(Erase heading not required.)*

Instructions regarding War Diaries and Intelligence Summaries are contained in F.S. Regs., Part II. and the Staff Manual respectively. Title pages will be prepared in manuscript.

| Place | Date | Hour | Summary of Events and Information | Remarks and references to Appendices |
|---|---|---|---|---|
| CRICOURT | 14/5/17 | | Early this morning our artillery caught a large body of Germans leaving LES TROIS SAUVAGES. The enemy have shelled heavily today & the enemy there are in the hit. The enemy fired a few grenades at our front line with T.M's and Rifle Grenades. | |
| " | 15/5/17 | | During the day everything was quiet. At night two companies of Sherwood Forester raided LES TROIS SAUVAGES. We had two casualties, two members in ranks died of wounds. After the raid the front was fairly quiet. | |
| | 16/5/17 | | This evening Pte Bleich No [ ] Z Coy behaved in a most gallant and daring manner. When it became doubly lighter Pte Bleich discovered that several Germans were lying between our advanced posts and LES TROIS SAUVAGES. Thinking that there were perhaps some of their wounded he went to see & then found out that seemingly wounded to clear | |

| Place | Date | Hour | Summary of Events and Information | Remarks and references to Appendices |
|---|---|---|---|---|
| GRICOURT | 16/9/17 | | Did a considerable amount of ground work to be thoroughly before he came up to the line not taking notice when he was under observation and being anxious one of the bullets going through the rim of his steel helmet. Who with 20 yds of the post he was unable to proceed further with the run. Pte Reed made his way back and soon the men were clear of he immediately came out from the main ones clear or he immediately went another more position to who survived. Everything was quiet during the day. | |
| KEEPERS LODGE | 17/9/17 | | All quiet during the day. Artillery activity during the night. No unusual activity during the day. Operations. Casualties for week ending twenty first Sept. Officer wounded J.L. Cripps -- wounds a rifle in front of pock. Casualties (other ranks) 1 killed 102 wounded. | |

Army Form C. 2118.

# WAR DIARY
## or
## INTELLIGENCE SUMMARY.
(Erase heading not required.)

Instructions regarding War Diaries and Intelligence Summaries are contained in F. S. Regs., Part II. and the Staff Manual respectively. Title pages will be prepared in manuscript.

| Place | Date | Hour | Summary of Events and Information | Remarks and references to Appendices |
|---|---|---|---|---|
| KEEPERS LODGE | 19/5/17 | | French advance parties were to our sector. Preparation for relief by the French. | |
| TERTRY | 20/5/17 | | The battalion was relieved by the French and reported the day and marched to TERTRY where the battalion was billeted. | |
| " | 21/5/17 | | Part of the day was spent in cleaning generally. In the afternoon the battalion bathed in CAULAINCOURT LAKE. In the morning training by companies & the evening baths opened. | |
| " | 22/5/17 | | Coy training and bathing in CAULAINCOURT LAKE. | |
| PERONNE | 23/5/17 | | The battalion marched to PERONNE. | |
| | 24/5/17 | | General inspection of camp by their O.C.s | |
| AIZECOURT LE BAS | 25/5/17 | | The battalion marched to AIZECOURT-LE-BAS when they were in bivouacs. | |
| | 26/5/17 | | Working party of 150 men worked at O.23.C. Specialists are in command of Corp. Stanley. | |

A 5834 Wt. W4973/M687 750,000 8/16 D. D. & L. Ltd. Forms/C.2118/13.

# WAR DIARY
## or
## INTELLIGENCE SUMMARY.

*(Erase heading not required.)*

Army Form C. 2118.

| Place | Date | Hour | Summary of Events and Information | Remarks and references to Appendices |
|---|---|---|---|---|
| AIZECOURT -LE-BAS | 27/5/17 | | Found working party of 100 men. Remainder of battalion on Speciales training. Church parade from 9 a.m. to 10 a.m. | |
| " | 28/5/17 | | Training by Coys, firing and training of specialists and operators of mortars. Working party of 100 men. | |
| " | 29/5/17 | | Do. Do. Do. | |
| " | 30/5/17 | | Do. Do. Do. | |
| " | 31/5/17 | | As usual. Working parties. Coys training firing a range. | |

W.P.S. Towell
Lieut. Col.
Comdg. 14th (S) Bn. Gloster Regt. (W. of E.)

To
105th Bde.

Herewith War Diary for the month of June.

W. S. S. Foord
................................................... Lieut. Col.
Comdg. 14th (S) Bn. Gloster Regt. (W. of E.)

8.7.17.

# WAR DIARY or INTELLIGENCE SUMMARY

Army Form C. 2118.

14 Gloucesters Vol 17

Comdg. 14th (S) Bn. Gloster Regt. (W. of E.)

| Place | Date | Hour | Summary of Events and Information | Remarks and references to Appendices |
|---|---|---|---|---|
| AIZECOURT-LE-BAS | 1/6/17 | | The battalion spent the day in training. Lieut. Spurrier having repeatedly neglected his duties as an advance party left to be attached to the 19th D.L.I. for purposes of recognising. In the evening owing to his conduct he had notice given to him that he would be returned to the 19th D.L.I. Regt. 2 other ranks on platoon of W. Coy to the base Y Corps appointments. | |
| " | 2/6/17 | | The afternoon the battalion marched to new area in VILLERS-GUISLAIN. The relief was carried out without incident. 2 O.Rs killed (attacked 10pdrs T.M.B) | |
| VILLERS-GUISLAIN | 3/6/17 | | Very quiet day in the line. VILLERS GUISLAIN shelled heavily during the whole of the day. The school hotel except for their gas room at noon. 1 O.R. killed. (Lc. Cpl Vander MM) | |
| " | 4/6/17 | | Steady artillery day. Wade returned on from leave. Casualties killed 2 O.Rs. wounded 1 O.R. | |
| " | 5/6/17 | | Quiet during the last 24 hrs. Own patrols reconnoitred the route of our front system. Enemy artillery very active during the evening. | |

**Army Form C. 2118.**

**WAR DIARY**
or
**INTELLIGENCE SUMMARY.**
*(Erase heading not required.)*

Comdg. 14th (S) Bn Gloster Regt. (W of E.)
Lieut. Col. ..........................

| Place | Date | Hour | Summary of Events and Information | Remarks and references to Appendices |
|---|---|---|---|---|
| VILLERS-GUISLAIN | 6/6/17 | | Enemy artillery active. We located two hostile guns. Considerable aerial activity by both sides. Considerable hostile officers! O.R.s. 2. | |
| " | 7/6/17 | | Our artillery very active today. Enemy planes attempted to cross our lines but were driven back by our A.A. guns. Considerable I.O.R. wounded. | |
| " | 8/6/17 | | Quiet during the last 24 hours. At night work on the front line trenches building shelters, moving general forward of trench. Considerable N.C. | |
| " | 9/6/17 | | Enemy artillery was fairly active. Our patrols cover the whole of the trench front. Work on a gun cover out on the front line. Considerable O.R.s. 1 killed 8 wounded. | |
| " | 10/6/17 | | During the day enemy artillery active. The late was relieved by 15th Sherwood Foresters. The relief was carried out without incident. Work was carried on during the night. Batt. in support. W.X.Y. coys were in the GREEN LINE Z coy in Villers Guislaine. Work was carried on and underholm experience of 9th R.E. & one coy worked in front of the GREEN LINE manning of trench. | |

# WAR DIARY
## or
## INTELLIGENCE SUMMARY

Army Form C. 2118.

| Place | Date | Hour | Summary of Events and Information | Remarks and references to Appendices |
|---|---|---|---|---|
| VILLERS-GUISLAIN | 12/6/17 | | Shells shelling not so heavy as usual on the village. Nothing particular was expression of R.E. Working parties – FRONT LINE - GREEN LINE also working parties – FRONT LINE. Casualties 1.O.R. wounded, 1 Officer wounded. | |
| " | 13/6/17 | | VILLERS GUISLAINS was heavily shelled during the day a great many of the shells ------- failed to explode. Wake men one on the 13/6/17. | |
| " | 14/6/17 | | Fair shelling to day. Aeroplane action a task rather went on yesterday. | |
| " | 15/6/17 | | Our guns were active during the day at night all any men working on a new trench in front of the old front line. VILLERS GUISLAINS sector | |
| " | 16/6/17 | | Practically no shelling but greats aerial activity then round the huts again somewhere as the men have been or- but strong. Do | |
| " | 17/6/17 | | Do | |
| " | 18/6/17 | | Slight shelling of VILLERS GUISLAINS at night. the batt now relieved by the 2nd Lancashire Fusiliers. & marched Camp H.N. of HEUDICOURT | |

E.S. Ward
Lieut. Col.
Comdg. 14th (S) Bn. ..................... A.I.F. of E.I.

Army Form C. 2118.

# WAR DIARY
## or
## INTELLIGENCE SUMMARY.
(Erase heading not required.)

| Place | Date | Hour | Summary of Events and Information | Remarks and references to Appendices |
|---|---|---|---|---|
| HEUDICOURT | 19/6/17 | | The hut opened the first day in Divisional Reserve in sleeping cups. | |
| " | 20/6/17 | | Working parties were found under supervision of 40th Division. 3 Coy BROWN LINE. 1 Coy R.E. | |
| " | 21/6/17 | | Working parties the same as yesterday. 1 Coy R.E. | |
| " | 22/6/17 | | Working parties as heretofore. HEUDICOURT. | |
| " | 23/6/17 | | Working parties as had as yesterday. Several officers and N.C.O.s attended a Bombing Demonstration at the Bombing School. | |
| " | 24/6/17 | | Working parties of 3 Coy BROWN LINE. 1 Coy R.E. under supervision of 40th Division. 1 Coy hut. | |
| " | " | | Do Do | |
| " | 25/6/17 | | 3½ Coys worked on BROWN LINE & Coy R.E. Under supervision of 40th Division. | |

Lieut. Col.
(W. of E.)
Comdg. 14th (S.)

B.S. Ford

Army Form C. 2118.

# WAR DIARY
### or
# INTELLIGENCE SUMMARY.
(Erase heading not required.)

| Place | Date | Hour | Summary of Events and Information | Remarks and references to Appendices |
|---|---|---|---|---|
| HEUDICOURT | 27/5/17 | | Day spent in cleaning up and preparing for line. At night the Bn relieved the 17th Royal Scots in Rt. front sub sector. The relief was carried out without incident. | |
| GAUCHE-WOOD | 28/5/17 | | Very quiet day. At night work commenced on NEW FRONT LINE deepening and strengthening all trenches generally. | |
| " | 29/5/17 | | Patrols shelled TURNER CRATER. CROOK QUARRY at intervals during the day. 2 Coys of 16th Cheshire Regt. worked on NEW FRONT LINE. X-Coy found covering patrols & their two coys. Craonville 2 O.R.c wounded | |
| " | 29/5/17 | | Shelling seen again took place rather more heavily than before. All coys worked on NEW FRONT LINE. Craonville 4 O.Rs. 2 coys of the 16th Cheshire Regt. worked as before. | |
| " | 30/5/17 | | Artillery shelling again very active on CROOK QUARRY. TURNER CRATER BROADHURST AVENUE WILLIS AVENUE and back old and new front line. Craonville 6 O.R.c wounded. | |

L.P.S. Frith
Lieut. Col.
Comdg. 14th (S) Bn. Gloster Regt. (W. of E.)

# WAR DIARY
## INTELLIGENCE SUMMARY

Army Form C. 2118.

105/35

14th (S) Bn Gloucester Regt.

Vol 18

Commdg. 14th (S) Bn. Gloster Regt. (W. of E.)
Sherwood Kelly, Lieut. Col.

| Place | Date | Hour | Summary of Events and Information | Remarks and references to Appendices |
|---|---|---|---|---|
| GAUCHE WOOD | 1/7/17 | | At 1.30 a.m. the enemy opened a heavy bombardment on back area NEW and OLD FRONT LINE, TURNER QUARRY, NEWTON POST, CROOK QUARRY. At the same time a barrage was put on WILLIS AVENUE, SUNKEN ROAD (McVAY ST.) BROADHURST AVENUE and TWENTY TWO RAVINE thus forming a Y shaped barrage. Both Coy H.Qs X & W Coys were subjected to a heavy bombardment. During the whole operation enemy intensity of the bombardment was very unreliable. Owing to the CROOK QUARRY lost telephone communication early in the action, what actually happened on their front cannot be ascertained. The left Coy H.Q, coy telephone communication was cut but were able to direct their artillery support. At 1.45 a.m. the barrage on the left lifted on to the garrison NEWTON POST were able to ask for gently getting through our wire. A heavy fire was brought to bear on these ... who were also Coy and rifle fire finished many of them. By luck particularly murderous affair on the wood, there were ... |  |

# WAR DIARY
## or
## INTELLIGENCE SUMMARY.

Army Form C. 2118.

| Place | Date | Hour | Summary of Events and Information | Remarks and references to Appendices |
|---|---|---|---|---|
| GAUCHE WOOD | 17/7/17 | | Cont'd. During this time another party made an attempt to get through on the left of NEWTON POST. Sgt. Bowie and Pte. Baldwin of X Coy left the trench and went at this party with the bayonet and succeeded in capturing one wounded man. The rest of the party dispersed. There was no sign of a attempted march on our RIGHT Coy (W). The bombardment ceased at 3.20 AM and recurred at 4.30 AM. Patrols went out after the raid but were unable to discover anything. During the day situation was normal. Casualties OR: 1 killed, 1 died of wounds & wounded. On the night of 17th July the batt. was relieved by the 21st Middlesex Regt. The relief was carried out without incident. When relieved Coys marched to the Peronne light railway when they entrained for camps VILLERS FAUCON. | |
| VILLERS FAUCON | 18/7/17 | | The day of July, 2 men spent in cleaning at (U.22.C). Coys all went to baths and Company training was carried out during the day. | |

# WAR DIARY
## or
## INTELLIGENCE SUMMARY

Army Form C. 2118.

| Place | Date | Hour | Summary of Events and Information | Remarks and references to Appendices |
|---|---|---|---|---|
| VILLERS FAUCON | 4/7/17 | | Company training was carried out. Lewis gunners had use of the ranges also. Next Coys. Specialists carried out training under specialist officers. | Stewart Lushly Lieut. Col. Comdg. 34th (S.) Bn Fusiliers Regt. (IV. of E.) |
| " | 5/7/17 | | Do. Do. Do. | |
| " | 6/7/17 | | Do. Do. Do. | |
| " | 7/7/17 | | In the morning training as before was carried out. In the afternoon the Batt. prepared to go into Reserve. It had took up its position in Reserve without incident. | |
| EPHEY | 8/7/17 | | The day was spent in building shelters. At night all Coys worked on NEW FRONT LINE. Work was proceeding up posts OSSUS 1, 2, 3 and 4. | |
| " | 9/7/17 | | Some work was carried out on the 8th July. All coys working on NEW FRONT LINE. Casualties 10 R wounded. | |

**Army Form C. 2118.**

# WAR DIARY
## or
## INTELLIGENCE SUMMARY.
*(Erase heading not required.)*

Instructions regarding War Diaries and Intelligence Summaries are contained in F. S. Regs., Part II. and the Staff Manual respectively. Title pages will be prepared in manuscript.

| Place | Date | Hour | Summary of Events and Information | Remarks and references to Appendices |
|---|---|---|---|---|
| EPHEY. | 11/7/17 | | Work was carried out on NEW FRONT LINE but was interrupted owing to enemy shelling. Casualties 1 O.R. Killed 2 O.Rs Wounded. | |
| " | 12/7/17 | | X Coy was attached to 108th Infantry Coy. 3 Coys at work on new trenches. Attempted raid by Germans on the BIRDCAGE. Coy occupied GREEN LINE. | |
| " | 13/7/17 | | No work was carried out to day. Casualties 2 Wounded. | |
| " | 14/7/17 | | Work as usual on new line by 3 Coys. No Casualties. | |
| " | 15/7/17 | | The Batt. was relieved by 17th Lancashire Fusiliers. The relief was carried out without incident. Coy when relieved marched back to Camp at Aizecourt-le-Bas. | |
| AIZE COURT-LE-BAS. | 16/7/17 | | Day spent in cleaning up and refitting. Coy under Coy commanders. Specialists under specialist officers. Class of officers & N.C.Os at Bde. H.Q. | |
| " | 17/7/17 | | Do Do Do | |
| " | 18/7/17 | | Do Do Do | |
| " | 19/7/17 | | Coy training in the morning & the afternoon in the attack. | |

Stewart Lloyd Lt Col
Comdg. 14th (S) Bn. Gloster Regt. (W. of E.)

**Army Form C. 2118.**

# WAR DIARY
## or
## INTELLIGENCE SUMMARY.
*(Erase heading not required.)*

Instructions regarding War Diaries and Intelligence Summaries are contained in F. S. Regs., Part II. and the Staff Manual respectively. Title pages will be prepared in manuscript.

Comdg. 14th (S.) Bn. Gloster Regt. (W. of E.)
Lieut. Col. Stanwell Wright.

| Place | Date | Hour | Summary of Events and Information | Remarks and references to Appendices |
|---|---|---|---|---|
| AIZECOURT-LE-BAS | 20/7/17 | | Coys training under Coy commanders. 2 Coys on Range. Class of officers & N.C.Os at Bn. H.Q. | |
| " | 21/7/17 | | Do Do Do | |
| " | 22/7/17 | | Training in the morning. 2 the afternoon a Rev. showing competition was held. Coy attended lecture at AIZECOURT-LE-BAS. | |
| LEMPIRE | 23/7/17 | | The morning was spent in cleaning and preparing for the line. At night the Bn. moved into the LEMPIRE sector. X coy in C post W coy in B post Y coy in A post. Z coy in reserve TOINE and ORCHARD posts. The relief was carried out without incident. We relieved 19th D.L.I. Casualties NIL. | |
| " | 24/7/17 | | Nothing important. Enemy patrols were out between posts. Casualties NIL. | |
| " | 25/7/17 | | General improvement of trenches during the day. Casualties NIL. | |

# WAR DIARY
## or
## INTELLIGENCE SUMMARY.

Army Form C. 2118.

| Place | Date | Hour | Summary of Events and Information | Remarks and references to Appendices |
|---|---|---|---|---|
| LEPPIRE | 26/7/17 | | Very quiet a few T.M.s were fired a C.M.T. POST. Although a considerable amount of shelling took place its never went across but. Casualties Nil. | |
| " | 27/7/17 | | Enemy rather more active C.M.T. POST shelled until T.M.s and a Light H.V. gun. Patrols were out and along the whole front from one of the enemy wire broadcasted. Wiring out. General improvement of trenches. Casualties Nil. | |
| " | 28/7/17 | | Few enemy activity. Never work a trenches. Casualties Nil. | |
| " | 29/7/17 | | Enemy mean quiet practically no hostile artillery activity. Work on mine and trenches. Patrols again out and a wiring front. no enemy encountered. Casualties Nil. | |
| " | 30/7/17 | | Practically no enemy activity. Usual work carried out at trench Patrols out along the whole of front. Casualties Nil. | |
| " | 31/7/17 | | Enemy artillery more active but improving. Work on patrols on usual Casualties Nil. | |

# WAR DIARY
## or
## INTELLIGENCE SUMMARY.

Army Form C. 2118.

14 Glouster Regt.
Vol 19

| Place | Date | Hour | Summary of Events and Information | Remarks and references to Appendices |
|---|---|---|---|---|
| LEMPIRE | 1/8/17 | | During the day very little hostile activity. At night the Battalion was relieved by 17th Royal Scots and 11th Suffolk Regt. "C" post was relieved by Royal Scots. "A" & "B" posts by Suffolk Regt. The relief was carried out without incident. On completion of relief Companies marched to camp at AIZECOURT-LE-BAS. Casualties NIL. | |
| AIZECOURT LE-BAS | 2/8/17 | | First day of Brigade in Reserve was spent in cleaning and Company kit inspections. | |
| " | 3/8/17 | | Companies training. All Companies had use of Bath. | |
| " | 4/8/17 | | Companies training. Bullet & Bayonet under Brigade instructors. | |
| " | 5/8/17 | | Companies training. Bullet & Bayonet under Brigade instructors. Brigade Church Parade was held on Brigade ground. After the service, medals were presented to officers and men of 105th Brigade and several men were congratulated for conspicuous gallantry by the Major General. | |
| " | 6/8/17 | | On conclusion of presentations Battalions marched by the G.O.C. 35th Division. | |
| " | 7/8/17 | | Companies training. Bullet and Bayonet under Brigade instructors. Two companies on range. | |
| " | 8/8/17 | | Companies training. All companies bathed. Companies training. Bullet and Bayonet. Two companies on range | |

L.17

**Army Form C. 2118.**

# WAR DIARY
## or
## INTELLIGENCE SUMMARY.
*(Erase heading not required.)*

Instructions regarding War Diaries and Intelligence Summaries are contained in F. S. Regs., Part II. and the Staff Manual respectively. Title pages will be prepared in manuscript.

Comdg. 14th (S) Bn. Gloster Regt. (IV a.r.)
Lieut. Col. ..................
E.J. Gad

| Place | Date | Hour | Summary of Events and Information | Remarks and references to Appendices |
|---|---|---|---|---|
| AIZECOURT-LE-BAS | 9/8/17 | | Battalion practise attack on the KNOLL. Bullet and Bayonet under Brigade instructor. | |
| " | 10/8/17 | | Companies training. Bullet and Bayonet Range. In the afternoon Brigade Sports were held. Casualties 1 O.R. wounded. | |
| " | 11/8/17 | | Companies training. Wiring. Bullet & Bayonet Range. | |
| " | 12/8/17 | | Church Parade on Brigade ground. Two companies wiring in the afternoon. | |
| " | 13/8/17 | | Companies training. Wiring practise, and making tanks concertina Wiring. Bullet & Bayonet under Brigade instructors. A party of bombers proceeded to LEMPIRE to detonate bombs. | |
| " | 14/8/17 | | Wiring. Bullet & Bayonet under Brigade instructors. | |
| " | 15/8/17 | | Wiring. Bullet & Bayonet. Battalion march through gas chamber. Casualties 1 O.R. gassed. | |
| " | 16/8/17 | | Two companies engaged on wiring and Bullet & Bayonet. Two companies marched to LEMPIRE. Battn. H.Q. at AIZECOURT-LE-BAS. | |
| " | 17/8/17 | | Two companies marched to camp in ST. EMELIE. Two companies in LEMPIRE. Battn. H.Q. moved to LEMPIRE. | |
| LEMPIRE | 18/8/17 | | Wire entanglements in preparation for the attack on the KNOLL, and carried out shoots on enemy emplacements. | |

Army Form C. 2118.

# WAR DIARY
## or
## INTELLIGENCE SUMMARY.
(Erase heading not required.)

Comdg: 14th (S) Bn. Gloster Regt. (W. of E.)
Lieut. Col. L.J. Bell

| Place | Date | Hour | Summary of Events and Information | Remarks and references to Appendices |
|---|---|---|---|---|
| LEMPIRE | 19/8/17 | | At 4 a.m. 105th Brigade carried out an attack on the KNOLL. All objectives were gained and the captured ground consolidated. At night all companies of the 14th Gloucester Regt. were engaged in wiring the new position, and a belt of wire erected along the whole of the new front. Casualties:- O.R. 1 killed, 4 wounded. | |
| " | 20/8/17 | | At night we relieved two companies of 15th Cheshires & 15th Sherwood Foresters on the KNOLL. The relief was carried out without incident. Casualties:- 1 officer wounded at duty. O.R.s wounded. | |
| KNOLL | 21/8/17 | | At 1 a.m. the enemy attempted to recapture the KNOLL. The attack was made at three separate points, assisted on the right by flammenwerfen. The enemy was repulsed at all points. During the day continuous shelling was kept up by hostile artillery. Casualties:- Officers, 1 killed, 1 wounded. O.R. 3 killed, 1 died of wounds, 16 wounded, 1 accidentally wounded and 1 wounded at duty. | |
| " | 22/8/17 | | During the day hostile artillery was much quieter; at night occasional bursts of fire were put on dumps, tracks, and | |

**Army Form C. 2218.**

# WAR DIARY
## or
## INTELLIGENCE SUMMARY.
*(Erase heading not required.)*

Instructions regarding War Diaries and Intelligence Summaries are contained in F. S. Regs., Part II. and the Staff Manual respectively. Title pages will be prepared in manuscript.

Remarks and references to Appendices

| Place | Date | Hour | Summary of Events and Information | Remarks |
|---|---|---|---|---|
| KNOLL | 22/8/17 | | roads leading to the line. The Battalion was relieved by 15th Cheshires and on relief "W" Company occupied E9o & FLEECEALL POSTS; "Y" Company GRAFTON POST; "X" Company, 1 platoon LEMPIRE EAST; 1 platoon LEMPIRE CENTRAL; remainder in billets. "Z" Company in billets in LEMPIRE. Casualties- O.R. 1 killed, 6 wounded. | |
| LEMPIRE | 23/8/17 | | During the day E9o POST slightly shelled at night "X" and "Z" Companies supplied carrying and wiring parties for the KNOLL. Casualties O.R. 2 wounded. | |
| " | 24/8/17 | | Covering parties were supplied by "W" & "Y" Companies for working parties at work on CRÉLLIN AVENUE & COCHRAN AVENUE, also carrying parties. Hostile shelling less than usual. Casualties NIL. | |
| " | 25/8/17 | | Enemy more active. E9o & FLEECEALL shelled heavily during enemy attack on GILLEMONT FARM. Working parties were clearing dugouts on the KNOLL. Casualties O.R. 1 killed, 1 Died of wounds, 5 wounded. | |
| " | 26/8/17 | | Enemy activity normal. Working parties on KNOLL under | |

Army Form C. 2118.

# WAR DIARY
## or
## INTELLIGENCE SUMMARY.
(Erase heading not required.)

| Place | Date | Hour | Summary of Events and Information | Remarks and references to Appendices |
|---|---|---|---|---|
| LEMPIRE | 26/8/17 27/8/17 | | Supervision of R.E's. Casualties O.R.1 killed 3 wounded. Covering parties were found for working parties. Enemy activity rather below normal. At night the Battalion was relieved by 17th West Yorkshire Regt. The relief was carried out without incident and on completion the Battalion marched to camp in VILLERS FAUCON. Casualties:- nil. | Comdg. 14th (S) Bn. D. York. Regt. (W. of E.) LAURIE, Col. |
| VILLERS-FAUCON | 28/8/17 | | Day was spent in clearing up and moving the camp to another site in VILLERS FAUCON. | |
| " | 29/8/17 30/8/17 | | Companies spent the day refitting, including one hour's musketry. Training was carried out in the morning. Two companies on range, and two at the disposal of Company Commanders. | |
| " | 31/8/17 | | The morning was spent in preparing to go into the line. Battalion moved to billets in LEMPIRE and were under the orders of the 106th Brigade. | |

Army Form C. 2118.

# WAR DIARY
## or
## INTELLIGENCE SUMMARY.
*(Erase heading not required.)*

Cmdg. 14th (S) Bn. Gloster Regt. (W.O.†B.)

14 Gloucesters Vol 20

| Place | Date | Hour | Summary of Events and Information | Remarks and references to Appendices |
|---|---|---|---|---|
| LEMPIRE | 1/9/17 | | During the day the Bn. was very quiet. At night the Bn relieved 19th D.L.I. in GUILLEMONT FM sector. The relief was carried out without incident. Casualties nil. | Miss Abrahams |
| | 2/9/17 | | During the day GUILLEMONT FM was shelled rather heavily with T.Ms. also CAT POST to which our artillery replied. Several work + improvements were carried out on Fr. trenches. Casualties 1 O.R. wounded. | |
| | 3/9/17 | | Again during the day CAT POST was shelled with T.Ms & 5.9s. Several direct hits were obtained on the post. Much however was repaired during the afternoon and night. It was quiet in the remainder of the Sector. Casualties 2 O.Rs killed & 2 O.Rs wounded. General work on trenches was carried out during the day. | B.S.S. Young |
| | 4/9/17 | | Was very quiet in the whole sector all day. Shortly after midnight CAT POST area again shelled with T.M.s & Artillery. Casualties nil. | |
| | 5/9/17 | | Very quiet during morning, but in the afternoon the enemy directed his attention to several track matters to assist throughout the remainder of the afternoon. Casualties nil. | L.H. |
| | 6/9/17 | | The day passed very quietly except for the occasional bursts of M.G. fire and the enemy's aeroplanes. The Battn. was relieved at dusk by the 10th Glouster Regt at night the Battn. marched with out incident by the 10th Glouster Regt. and marched back to camp at Emilie ............ | |

Army Form C. 2118.

# WAR DIARY
## or
## INTELLIGENCE SUMMARY.
*(Erase heading not required.)*

Instructions regarding War Diaries and Intelligence Summaries are contained in F.S. Regs., Part II and the Staff Manual respectively. Title pages will be prepared in manuscript.

| Place | Date | Hour | Summary of Events and Information | Remarks and references to Appendices |
|---|---|---|---|---|
| ST EMILIE | 7/9/17. | | The Battalion spent the day in cleaning of equipment and inspections. Casualties nil. | |
| " | 8/9/17. | | Two companies were employed making barbed entanglements during the day which were taken up to the line at night when the wiring was done by the two companies who were resting by day. Casualties nil. | |
| " | 9/9/17. | | Wiring was again done by two companies. The other two companies worked during the day making barbed wire entanglements. Casualties nil. | |
| " | 10/9/17. | | Three "X" companies were employed making barbed entanglements during morning and during the afternoon the other two companies also made concertina wire. At night the companies again marched to line and were employed wiring the night. Casualties nil. | |
| " | 11/9/17. | | The day was spent in cleaning up the camp generally, and at 5 pm Batn marched back to camp at AIZECOURT-LE-BAS taking over the camp from the 17th Lancashire Fusiliers. Casualties nil. | |
| AIZECOURT LE BAS | 12/9/17. | | During the day the companies and platoons commanders had a thorough inspection of all Lewis Guns, Bombs, Ammunition, men carried on. Casualties nil. | |

Commdg. 14th (S) Bn. Chester Regt. (W. of E.)
Lieut. Col.

S. J. Leaf

# WAR DIARY
## or
## INTELLIGENCE SUMMARY.

Army Form C. 2118.

| Place | Date | Hour | Summary of Events and Information | Remarks and references to Appendices |
|---|---|---|---|---|
| AIRECOURT LE-BAS | 13/9/17 | | During the day boys training on the ranges, and Bullet & Bayonet under Bloyets instructors. Recreation during the afternoon, 6th Bucks and football matches being played. Casualties nil. | |
| | 14/9/17 | | All companies training during the day. Bullet & Bayonet under Bloyets instructors. Lectures, drill, and musketry on the ranges. Casualties nil. | |
| | 15/9/17 | | Training under company commanders, Platoon and Bayonet also Lewis & Bayonet in Brigade under Bde instructors. Casualties nil. | |
| | 16/9/17 | | A Brigade church parade and inspection were held in the morning, followed by a Bde and engagement inspection by Coy commanders. Recreation during the afternoon. Casualties nil. | Pte A Bunce & MM Sept 6 Lt Shuttleworth MC<br>Sgt Battin MM<br>Pte Keeling MM<br>Pte Pittway MM<br>Pte Crutchley MM were distributed (?) |
| | 17/9/17 | | A Brigade parade was held at which Medal Ribbons & 3 men in the Bn received Military Medals and 2 Officers work the Military Cross. Football & cricket during the afternoon. Casualties nil. | |
| | 18/9/17 | | The morning was spent cleaning the camp and at 3.30pm moved off and relieved the 1st Highland Light Infantry in the left sub sector of the HONNECOURT area. Bn: The Entrance (?) | |
| EPEHY | 19/9/17 | | General work in trenches during the day. VILLERS GUISLAIN shelled slightly in the day. Casualties nil. | |

Comdg. 2/4th (S) Bn. Gloster Regt (W.N.E.)

Army Form C. 2118.

# WAR DIARY
## or
## INTELLIGENCE SUMMARY.
*(Erase heading not required.)*

| Place | Date | Hour | Summary of Events and Information | Remarks and references to Appendices |
|---|---|---|---|---|
| EPEHY. | 20/9/17. | | General work was carried out on the trenches during the day. The front line was shelled lightly at the junction of FAUCUS AVE. They quiet on rest of sector all day. Patrol visited enemies wire during the night and found this to be in good condition and rather deep. Casualties Nil. | |
| " | 21/9/17. | | General work in trenches, wiring and drainage. Front line shelled very lightly during the morning. In the afternoon VILLERS GUISLAIN was shelled steadily until dusk. Casualties Nil. | |
| " | 22/9/17. | | Work in Support Line and Green Line during the day. Also wiring and drainage of FAUCUS AVENUE. E.A's very active wiring on land at intervals during the day. Casualties Nil. | |
| " | 23/9/17. | | Work under R.E. supervision. Drainage and wiring of STORAR AVE also work on shelters and pumps etc in Front Line trench. Dying Room and Gun Post Star commenced in GLOSTER ROAD under R.E. officer. Casualties Nil. | |
| " | 24/9/17. | | General work carried out on trenches both front line and Support during the day, further work needed. R.E. supervision on Gun Post Star and Dying Room in GLOSTER Rd. E.A's very active all day crossing our line singly and in pairs. Casualties Nil. | |
| " | 25/9/17. | | Work in Front Line and STORAR AVENUE during the day also parties as on previous days working under R.E. supervision on Shelters in Scotch Road. Enemy artillery active on areas behind the line during the day presumably counter Battery work. Casualties Nil. | |

Comdg. 1/4th (S) Bn. Gloster Regt (T. of L.)
Lieut. Col.
[signature]

**Army Form C. 2118.**

# WAR DIARY
## or
## INTELLIGENCE SUMMARY.
*(Erase heading not required.)*

Instructions regarding War Diaries and Intelligence Summaries are contained in F. S. Regs., Part II. and the Staff Manual respectively. Title pages will be prepared in manuscript.

Comdg. 1st/5th Bn. Chester Regt. (W. of L.)

Lieut. Col.
G. S. Brighten

| Place | Date | Hour | Summary of Events and Information | Remarks and references to Appendices |
|---|---|---|---|---|
| EPEHY. | 26/9/17. | | It was very quiet on the whole of the Bn. Sector all day. Work was carried out on Front Support & Reserve Line during the day. Small parties were allowed to march from Fifth Avenue and Baths in Green Road about 70 men bathed during the day. Casualties Nil. | |
| " | 27/9/17. | | The usual work was carried out in the Trenches during the day. Also Lewis Gun posts Saps & Shelters in Green Road under R.E. About 50 men from Company's bathed during the day. E.A.'s very active throughout the day. Casualties Nil. Work on CHORD TRENCH during this night. | |
| " | 28/9/17. | | In places where the new earth was plainly visible, owing to the work during the night on CHORD TRENCH the enemy fired on this place with Rifle Grenades and Lewis in the day shelled it lightly. General Work on Front and Support Lines during the day. Casualties Nil. | |
| " | 29/9/17. | | A fighting patrol of 2 O.H. + 25 O.Rs. went out to the crater on CANNON GATE Rd at about 1 A.M. They moved up under cover of a mist. Unfortunately the mist lifted when they were within about 50 x of the enemy wire exposing them to view. The enemy then booked in front of the own wire and opened heavy rifle + M.G. fire. Several attempts were made to rush Bungalows but this was impossible owing to M.G. fire. At times the enemy ran from his trench to his wire and threw bombs. Our patrol fired on these and 3 enemy were known to fall also this wire apparently down and several more wounded were hurried back to the Trench probably wounded. Our casualties were 1 Off + 4 O.Rs. wounded. Usual Work on Trenches during the day. | |
| " | 30/9/17. | | It was very quiet on the whole of the Bn. Sector throughout the day. At night the Bn. was relieved without incident by the 1st/5th Loyal North Lancashire Regiment, and marched to to Billets in VILLERS FAUCON. Casualties Nil. | |

35/105

Army Form C. 2118.

# WAR DIARY
## or
## INTELLIGENCE SUMMARY.
*(Erase heading not required.)*

Army Form C. 2118.

14th Bn. Gloster Regiment.
October 1917.

Vol 27

Commdg. 14th (S) Bn. Gloster Regt. (W. of F.)
............................ Lieut. Col.

L. 19

| Place | Date | Hour | Summary of Events and Information | Remarks and references to Appendices |
|---|---|---|---|---|
| Villers Faucon | 1/10/17 | | The Battalion moved from Bullik to Villers Faucon by Lorry to Peronne. Branaltis tue. | |
| Peronne | 2/10/17 | | During the morning Draft when joined the battalion in the last hunk were inspected by the G.O.C. Companies spent the day generally cleaning up equipment etc. Inspection by Company Officers of Arms Equipment etc. Branaltis tue. | |
| | 3/10/17 | | The battalion was inspected by the Commanding Officer in the morning. At 7.40 pm the battalion was entrained to the Peronne-Flamicourt Station and entrained at about 1.30 am for Arras. Branaltis tue. | Food S.D.9 |
| Arras | 4/10/17 | | The battalion arrived at about 6.30am, formed up and marched to billets in Dainville. Branaltis tue. | |
| Dainville | 5/10/17 | | Remainder of day rested. Branaltis tue. Battalion parade and inspection by Commanding Officer & arms drill in the morning. Draft tested in Musketry & Lewis Lighting remainder, period arms drill under Platoon Commanders, Lewis Gun, Revolver, and Rifle Grenade practice under their respective officers. Range Practice & Gas Drill was also carried out. 760s in ammunition drill & fire direction. Branaltis tue. | |
| | 6/10/17 | | Training under Platoon Commanders Range Practice, and Lewis Gunners, Repre... [illegible] under Platoon Officers. Branaltis tue. | |

**Army Form C. 2118.**

# WAR DIARY
## or
## INTELLIGENCE SUMMARY.

*(Erase heading not required.)*

Lieut. Col. .......................... Comdg. 14th (S) Bn. Gloster Regt. (W. of E.)

| Place | Date | Hour | Summary of Events and Information | Remarks and references to Appendices |
|---|---|---|---|---|
| DAINVILLE | 7/10/17 | | Section Training under Section Commanders & Battalion Parade in the morning. Training in Skill at Arms Section in Fire Control, Fire discipline, and the assault. Rifle Section, Bombing Sections, Lewis Gun Sections, and Rifle Grenade Sections training as laid down in SS 152. Casualties nil. | |
| | 8/10/17 | | Battalion Parade in morning. Musketry and Range practices and Skill at Arms and L.G. Bombing & Rifle Grenade Sections under their respective Officers. Casualties nil. | |
| | 9/10/17 | | Battalion Parade in morning under Commanding Officer. Individual training Skill at Arms. Platoon Training was held in the afternoon, the Platoons in the attack. Range practices, Gas Drill in the afternoon. N.C.Os. Training in Commanding Drill & Fire Direction. Casualties nil. | |
| | 10/10/17 | | Lewis Gun Training, Bombing & Rifle Grenade training under their respective Officers. Platoon Training, and Platoon in the attack under Platoon Officers. Connected Files. | |
| | 11/10/17 | | Platoon drill under Platoon Officers. Signallers and Runners under Signal Officer. Stretcher Bearers & Sanitary men under Medical Officer during the morning. Return by Company Commanders during the afternoon. Casualties nil. | |
| | 12/10/17 | | Battalion Parade in morning. Lewis Gun, Bombing, & Rifle Grenade Section under their respective Officers. Stretcher Bearers under Medical Officer. Casualties nil. | |

Army Form C. 2118.

# WAR DIARY
# or
# INTELLIGENCE SUMMARY.
(Erase heading not required.)

Instructions regarding War Diaries and Intelligence Summaries are contained in F. S. Regs., Part II. and the Staff Manual respectively. Title pages will be prepared in manuscript.

Comdg. 14th (S) Bn. Gloster Regt. (W. of E.)
Lieut. Col. ...................................

| Place | Date | Hour | Summary of Events and Information | Remarks and references to Appendices |
|---|---|---|---|---|
| DAINVILLE | 13/10/17 | | Battalion left DAINVILLE marching away at 6 am and arrived at ARRAS where Battalion entrained at 8.45 am for BAVINCHOVE this they detrained at 2.40 pm and marched to LEDRINGHEM arriving there at 6.30 pm. Casualties nil. | |
| LEDRINGHEM | 14/10/17 | | The day was spent cleaning equipment + Kit etc. Inspection by Company Commanders. Casualties nil. | |
| | 15/10/17 | | The Battalion marched from LEDRINGHEM at 8.30 am and arrived at ARNEKE at 9.50 am when Battn entrained at 10.15 am and left at 11.30 am for PROVEN. Battalion arrived at PROVEN at 2.30 pm when they detrained and marched to P.H. Camp arriving there at 11.06 pm. Casualties nil. | |
| PROVEN | 16/10/17 | | Battalion marched over from P.H. Camp to Station and entrained at 11.30 am for ELVERDINGHE. Battn. arrived at ELVERDINGHE at 12.30 when they detrained and marched to LARREY Camp arriving there at 1.15 pm. Billets in NISSEN HUTS. Casualties nil. | |
| ELVERDINGHE | 17/10/17 | | Inspection by Platoon Commanders of mens Kits and equipment etc. Bombers & Running were also Lewis Gunners were inspected by respective Instructors. Casualties nil. | |
| | 18/10/17 | | Inspection by the G.O. Division in the morning. Lewis Gun and Bombing Sections exercised by respective Commanders. etc. | |

# WAR DIARY
## or
## INTELLIGENCE SUMMARY

Army Form C. 2118.

Comdg. 14th (S) Bn. Gloster Regt. (W. of E.)
................................... Lieut. Col.

| Place | Date | Hour | Summary of Events and Information | Remarks and references to Appendices |
|---|---|---|---|---|
| HOUTHULST FOREST. | 22/10/17 | | At 12 m/n the Batt. was in position of assembly for the attack. Rain fell intermittently but the men were in splendid spirits. At 4.30 a.m. a rum ration was issued. The barrage opened at 5.35 a.m. and our leading Coys moved up as close to the barrage as possible. The barrage, however, was at an advance of about 10 yards in a minute, and was very difficult to keep up with. The Coys moved out eventually. The appropriate centre of the first objective was reached. The left Coy. not met by heavy enemy gun fire from PANAMA HOUSE. Cpt. Ronan immediately led a party against it, though only one man was left unwounded. Richly manner a killing 2 officers and 5 men, taken about 20 others occupants. Then tried to escape, but were killed by other parties. By the first time — then near Captainvood. Skirmishes continued but 6.20 am the left Coys had taken its first objective. Meanwhile the centre Coys taken its first objective, and a further 5.IAIprisoners. The right Coy was experiencing some difficulty in keeping up, its advance being very much hampered by snipers. Capt W Bakel M.C. commander of its rear Coy, was also wounded about the same time on his left. A new Coy of Captain FJS Quayle was being carried on with great vigour. Eventually all objectives were not firm and at the final objective was held. | T J Ford |

# Army Form C. 2118.

## WAR DIARY
## or
## INTELLIGENCE SUMMARY.
(Erase heading not required.)

| Place | Date | Hour | Summary of Events and Information | Remarks and references to Appendices |
|---|---|---|---|---|
| HOULTHULST FOREST | | | This night Coy Hd. lunch with the entire coy away to following the night. Both which used too far to its right. This did not with opposition and reached the first objective without difficulty. The support Coy had in the meantime advanced hither to handy company was now in positions close behind by leading coys of the North Co. across the situation at 6.16 a.m. the Battalion had successfully occupied its first objective though the support coy was only if could be afterwards of try detachments to the front position. The left coy was again hit up at the gap but the left flank of the tills already atypical where they also met with some difficulty. Gradually Capt Revell such a small party attempted an advance forward and came on the remainder of the coy more or later under a latter and by 7:30 a.m. the faraline were on the second objective. This coy now on the first to reach its final objective. The chance went ahead so up pushed on to our relaxation that coy up to the operations pushed most strongly assisted attempt to move forward with its intentional attention to our left company. Consequently advance was held up and also and probable made a hosting point. The same time late advance in advance with the 10th Division commenced now being thrown up will three up by a pill box cleanly expediting the advance of our right flank. | |

Commdg. 14th (S) Bn. Gloster Regt. (W. C/ E.).
Lieut.-Col.

# WAR DIARY or INTELLIGENCE SUMMARY

Army Form C. 2118.

*Commdg. 14th (S) Bn. Gloster Regt. (W. of E.)*
*Lieut. Col.* .................................................

| Place | Date | Hour | Summary of Events and Information | Remarks and references to Appendices |
|---|---|---|---|---|
| HOUTHULST FOREST | | | The enemy on our immediate front offered little resistance except at one pill-box approx U.6.a.1.6. where a/c fire was encountered. By abt 7.45 A.M. our two right Coys had reached their final objectives while the support Coy not meeting with resistance passed straight on to Consolidate the line PANAMA — COLOM R.C. Our platoon strength was weakened by casualties (17 men being killed by an a/c) and our 4 Coys were composed well under to meet over the first line. The Enemy did not appear to be in great strength except at the Land's End Corner of the wood where some of the heads were flung. Our pill-boxes were extremely stoutly however what opposition we forward except in some specified the offensive hastily pilling hats did more and more machine gun fire on forth front. At 7.45 A.M. all corps had installed and any objective had consolidated on the object have been lost together. There was arrived. Capt Rendall took charge of the his ability to obtain the wire  as apparently the attempts to take arriving of his disposition. Considering the highly concentrated. Getting the front line very weak he brought up the support Coy, supplying up our any men strength he could before strengthen it and at over Part about the consolidation of the attack. At 8 A.M. a Coy of the 15th SHERWOOD FORESTERS (reserve behind LOUVOIS Fm) was sent up to support in close position behind PANAMA Frm in our —— H.Q. |

A5834  Wt W4973/MG57  732,000  8/16  D. D. & L. Ltd Forms/C2118/18  B H.Q.

| Place | Date | Hour | Summary of Events and Information | Remarks and references to Appendices |
|---|---|---|---|---|
| HOUTHULST FOREST | | | Meanwhile Capt. Russell had gone along to get our snipers to find out the position of the enemy battalion. After our artillery barrage went on, truth with them was enough to our night and also after, in view of his return he reported all activities to the officer commanding the end of the platoon to join the gap. The content of this officer Capt. Henry MC (11th Sherwood Foresters) was splendid throughout the danger on the occasions he showed an invaluable. It was hoped this platoon could be brought further in accord of the flank - difficulty ??? ment out the activity of enemy snipers, many things seriously dangerous to escape amidst the enemy fire of enemy being advantage to erring the locality well down the POTTE DRIEF mud in front of us was Camouflaged screen affording them exceptt cover on very their artistic plans provided in addition the ???? fire, they were able to snipe [???] be highly valuable by all offices by Capt Russell + Henry had managed to ???? the ???? that sniping he had proved with two offices have been constantly ??? their effects on their powers of organization had shown up splendidly. | 6 P S read |

# WAR DIARY
## or
## INTELLIGENCE SUMMARY.

*(Erase heading not required.)*

Army Form C. 2118.

Comdg. 14th (S) Bn. Gloster Regt. (W.G.R.)
Lieut: Col.

| Place | Date | Hour | Summary of Events and Information | Remarks and references to Appendices |
|---|---|---|---|---|
| 4th AUGUST FOREST | | | So much for the actual battle front. Further back the enemy's artillery had been very active assisted by aeroplane observation. Bn. H.Q. was shelled for 2 hrs and received two direct hits, and a barrage was kept at intervals just behind our old front line. the vicinity of the Regt. Aid Post was also shelled continuously all day. Enemy aircraft were very numerous flying low, replying on appeared to the movements by our planes. The situation remained unchanged until about 4.15 p.m. when the enemy counter barrage to about the same area, apparently the attack on Courcelet and artillery barrage. A very friendly intercepted a Tank might have turned the scale and given us possession back to the Southern edge of the wood. This Btn. on now night flank in a very defence condition. Capt. Blundell with all approved withdrew part of his from there at (place?) than in echelon back to the Sunken road of the wood to join up with the new ferries of the right Left to do this another platoon of the SHERWOOD FORESTERS was required owing to veranda length of his line and safely the new formation was made when the enemy were by noticed by Capt. Blundell. However were called. Nothing of interest occurred. | |

Army Form C. 2118.

# WAR DIARY
## or
## INTELLIGENCE SUMMARY.
(Erase heading not required.)

Instructions regarding War Diaries and Intelligence Summaries are contained in F. S. Regs., Part II. and the Staff Manual respectively. Title pages will be prepared in manuscript.

(Comdg. 14th (S) Bn. Gloster Regt. (W. of E.))
Lieut. Col. ..........................

| Place | Date | Hour | Summary of Events and Information | Remarks and references to Appendices |
|---|---|---|---|---|
| ELVERDINGHE | 19/10/17 | | General equipment of Platoons for offensive action. Inspection of Platoons in fighting order by Platoon Commanders. Casualties 1 O.R. Wounded. | |
| " | 20/10/17 | | General fatigue work during the day & Inspection by Platoon & Company Commanders. Casualties 1 O.R. Wounded. At night the Battalion relieved the 19th Highland Light Infantry. Regiment | |
| HOULTHULST FOREST | 21/10/17 | | Hostile shelling quiet during the night. At 5.15am the enemy put down a heavy barrage which lasted ½ an hour. Hostile artillery fairly quiet during the day. Hostile Aircraft very active flying low and firing a great deal with machine guns. At 5p enemy shelling increased & continued intermittently during the night. The Batt. assembly was complete by 11 p.m. | |

E.S. 1994

**WAR DIARY**
or
**INTELLIGENCE SUMMARY.**

(Erase heading not required.)

Army Form C. 2118.

| Place | Date | Hour | Summary of Events and Information | Remarks and references to Appendices |
|---|---|---|---|---|
| LARREY CAMP | 24.10.17 | | Battalion entrained from BOESINGHE to ELVERDINGHE where they detrained and marched to LARREY CAMP, where Rations were killed in troops huts Baraillie Hill | |
| " | 25.10.17 | | The whole day was spent in the cleaning of clothes, equipment, & Kit. The heavy feet were rubbed with whale oil. Baraillie Hill. | |
| " | 26.10.17 | | The day was spent in cleaning Kit, Equipment inspection and inspection by Platoon Commanders. During the evening 1 shell was fired in the camp falling between A Huts Baraillie, 2 ORs killed, 16 ORs Wounded, 1 OR wounded at duty. | |
| " | 27.10.17 | | Inspections by Platoon Commanders, Various parties were detailed to work on the improvement of Camp. Sandbagging the outside of Huts was commenced Baraillie Hill. | |
| " | 27.10.17 | | Sandbagging of the outside of Huts was continued, and Duckboard tracks were laid down from huts to the road. Inspection by Platoon Commanders Baraillie Hill | |
| " | 28.10.17 | | Church of England parade and Holy Communion was held in the morning. Kit and equipment inspection by Platoon Commanders. General improvement of Camp Baraillie Hill | |

Comdg. 14th (S) Bn. Gloster Regt., I.W., A.E.F.
Lieut. Col.

E.S. Lloyd

Army Form C. 2118.

# WAR DIARY
## or
## INTELLIGENCE SUMMARY.
*(Erase heading not required.)*

14th (S) Bn. Gloster Regt. (W. of E.)
Lieut. Col.
L.J. Reed

| Place | Date | Hour | Summary of Events and Information | Remarks and references to Appendices |
|---|---|---|---|---|
| LARREY CAMP. | 29/10/17 | | Platoons were inspected by their respective commanders in the morning. At about 4 p.m. Battalion moved off by Platoons to relieve the 7K Lincoln Regt. Relief was completed by 9.30 p.m. and was carried out without incident. Casualties 2 O.Rs Wounded in Action. | |
| HOUTHULST FOREST | 30/10/17 | | Hostile shelling was regularly kept up during the day on LOUVOIS FARM and PANAMA HOUSE. At 6 p.m. a barrage was put along our Corps Front as a diversion for the attack of the Division on our Right. It was very quiet during the night. Our patrols were unable to get in effect with the enemy at any point. Casualties :- 1 Officer Wounded, 1 O.R. Killed, and 4 O.Rs. wounded. | |
| | 31/10/17 | | During the day our guns were very quiet. Hostile shelling of Back Areas was continued throughout the day. At night a barrage was put on JUDGES Cr. and NEY WOOD. There was no usual shelling on our front. Again our patrols were unable to get in contact with the enemy at any point. Casualties :- 1 O.R. Killed, 10 O.R. Wounded. | |

# WAR DIARY

## INTELLIGENCE SUMMARY. 14th (S) Bn. Gloster Regiment

*(Contd. 14th (S) Bn. Gloster Regt. (W. of E.))*

Lieut Col — Major Bevan

| Place | Date | Hour | Summary of Events and Information | Remarks and references to Appendices |
|-------|------|------|-----------------------------------|-------|
| HOUTHULST FOREST | 1/11/17 | | During the day hostile artillery was very active behind the Line. LOUVOIS FARM and BLORGES STREET was shelled at intervals mostly by 4.2, and 5.9" shells. At night the Battalion was relieved by the 17th Royal Scots. During the relief CLARGES STREET was shelled heavily with Gas shells and H.E. Tea was provided for the men at BOESINGHE STATION, where Battn entrained for ONDANK. Here they detrained and marched to Billets in DYKE CAMP. Casualties 2 O.Rs. Killed & 8 O.Rs. Wounded. | |
| DYKE CAMP | 2/11/17 | | Battalion rested during the day. Lect inspection by Medical Officers in the afternoon. Casualties nil. | |
| " | 3/11/17 | | Battalion bathing from 9am to 11am at ELVERDINGHE CHATEAU. Inspection of feet by Medical Officer in the afternoon. Casualties nil. | |
| " | 4/11/17 | | Protective measures against hostile aircraft were elaborated during the day by various working parties. Inspection of Draft by Medical Officer in the afternoon. Casualties nil. | |
| " | 5/11/17 | | At 11:30am Battalion paraded and marched off by companies to ONDANK STATION where Battn entrained for PROVEN. Here they detrained and marched to PENTON CAMP. Casualties nil. | |

Army Form C. 2118.

# WAR DIARY
# INTELLIGENCE SUMMARY. 14th (S) Bn. Gloster Regiment.

(Erase heading not required.)

Instructions regarding War Diaries and Intelligence Summaries are contained in F.S. Regs., Part II. and the Staff Manual respectively. Title pages will be prepared in manuscript.

| Place | Date | Hour | Summary of Events and Information | Remarks and references to Appendices |
|---|---|---|---|---|
| PENTON CAMP | 6/10/17 | | Arms drill and musketry during the morning. Feet inspection by Medical Officer in the afternoon. Various fatigue parties were engaged on drainage of camp throughout the day. Bawdsey hill. | |
| " | 7/10/17 | | The morning was devoted to general training. 1 hour Arms drill, 1½ hours musketry and range practice and parade for the rubbing of feet with whale oil. Protective measures against hostile aircraft were continued. Bawdsey hill. | |
| " | 8/10/17 | | Inspections by Platoon Commanders. Musketry on Range. Arms drill and Physical exercise during the morning. Recreation during the afternoon. Bawdsey hill. | |
| " | 9/10/17 | | General training between hours of 9 am and 12.30 pm including Range practice. Recreation during the afternoon. Bawdsey hill. | |
| " | 10/10/17 | | Battalion exchanged camps with 17th H.L.I. Companies moved off independently to PETWORTH CAMP exchange was completed by 12.30 pm. Recreation during afternoon. Bawdsey hill. | |
| PETWORTH CAMP | 11/10/17 | | Training was carried out as at Penton Camp from 9 am to 12.30 pm. Football match during the afternoon. In the evening 200 O.R.s visited Cinema Hall PROVEN. Bawdsey hill. | |
| " | 12/10/17 | | Training as on previous day. The last 30 minutes being devoted to Battalion drill. Recreation during the afternoon. 160 O.Rs visited Cinema Hall Proven in the evening. Bawdsey hill. | |

Commde. 14th (S) Bn. Gloster Regt. (W. of E.)
Lieut. Col.
B. J. Ford

Army Form C. 2118.

# WAR DIARY
## or
## INTELLIGENCE SUMMARY. 14th (S) Bn. Gloster Regiment

(Erase heading not required.)

Instructions regarding War Diaries and Intelligence Summaries are contained in F.S. Regs., Part II. and the Staff Manual respectively. Title pages will be prepared in manuscript.

Commdg. 14th (S) Bn. Gloster Regt. (S.W. of E.)
Lieut. Col. ————————————
Lt C. Ford

| Place | Date | Hour | Summary of Events and Information | Remarks and references to Appendices |
|---|---|---|---|---|
| PETWORTH CAMP | 13/11/17 | | Training was carried out during the hours 9 am to 12.30 pm at conclusion of morning's parade Battalion marched past Commanding Officer. Recreation during the afternoon. Battalion Trid. | |
| " | 14/11/17 | | During the day training as on previous days. Lecture by bombing instructor. Football match in the afternoon. 200 ORs visited Cinema Hall, Proven, Battalion Trid. | |
| " | 15/11/17 | | Battalion marched from Petwork Camp at 8.46' to PROVEN and entrained for ONDANK Station, the Battn detrained there and marched to F and X Camp, arrived there at 11.46 am. Recreation during the afternoon. Battalion Trid. | |
| "FQX" Camp | 16/11/17 | | During the day training was carried out between the hours of 9 am and 12.30 pm at conclusion of march the Battalion marched past Commanding Officer. the afternoon devoted to Sports & Games. Battalion Trid. | |
| | 17/11/17 | | Training as on previous days, 9 am to 12.30 pm the Battn 30 mark Battalion will curries Commanding Officer. Football during the afternoon. Battalion Trid. | |
| | 18/11/17 | | Training as on previous days. In the afternoon the General Commanding the Division presented Medal Ribbonds to the Sta. M.M. to Sgt. Long, Pte's Burgett, Blakes, Cork and | |

# WAR DIARY
## INTELLIGENCE SUMMARY. 1/4 (S) Bn. Gloster Regiment

Army Form C. 2118.

| Place | Date | Hour | Summary of Events and Information | Remarks and references to Appendices |
|---|---|---|---|---|
| F. & X. Camp | 19/10/17 | | Training during the morning, Range practice, and Bayonet Bournameout course Football match in the afternoon Bournailles tue. | |
| | 20/10/17 | | As on previous days the hours 9 am to 12.30 pm and also 5 to General Training the last half hour of parade were spent in Battalion drill under Commanding Officer. Bournailles tue | |
| | 21/10/17 | | Inspection by Platoon and Company Commanders. Arms drill. Physical Training and Bayonet Training throughout the morning. Recreation during the afternoon. Bournailles tue. | |
| | 22/10/17 | | Battalion bathing during the morning also training was carried out until 12.30 pm. A football match between players in the afternoon Bournailles tue. | |
| | 23/10/17 | | There were a Brigade parade in the morning at which the Divisional Commander presented Medal Ribands to Officers & O.R. of the bgde. M.C. to Capt A.K. Will and M.M. to Sergt. Joy. At conclusion of presentation the Brigade marched past the General by Battalions. Remainder of day were spent in preparation for the line. Bournailles tue. | |
| | 24/10/17 | | At 1 pm the Battalion marched from Camp into respre. Two Companies were billeted at CANAL BANK and the remaining bays at KEMPTON PARK. The latter worked under R.A. being in charge of Major S.A. Parker. The relief was carried out without incident. Bournailles tue. | |

Lieut. Col.
Comdg. 1/4th (S) Bn. Gloster Regt. (W. of E.)

Army Form C. 2118.

# WAR DIARY
## or
## INTELLIGENCE SUMMARY. 1/4th (S) Bn. Gloster Regiment.
(Erase heading not required.)

Commdg. 1/4th (S) Bn. Gloster Regt. (W. of E.)
..................................... Lieut. Col.
W.F. Ford

| Place | Date | Hour | Summary of Events and Information | Remarks and references to Appendices |
|---|---|---|---|---|
| CANAL BANK. | 25/4/17 | | The day passed with the usual artillery activity along the front which however increased towards evening. There was a ceremonial church parade at the Bucket Abbey that was Canal Bank. Casualties Nil. | |
| " | 26/4/17 | | The two companies on CANAL BANK supplied various working parties to R.E. during the day. Artillery activity on both sides continued throughout the day. Casualties 1 O.R. wounded in action. | |
| " | 27/4/17 | | Usual artillery activity throughout the day. On account of improved weather, & as became marked active, flying very low over ST JULIEN about noon. Shortly afterwards a formation of 6 E.A's passed over ST JEAN flying very high in the direction of YPRES. Between the hours of 10 am and 12 noon the area about CONSULATE FARM was shelled with heavy shrapnel. The Australian Balloon west of ST JEAN was also shelled and about 4 pm Casualties hill. | |
| " | 28/4/17 | | During the morning about 30 rounds of shrapnel were fired at the Observation Balloon N.E of BRIELEN. At 1 pm about 300 men who were stationed on CANAL BANK returned a sunday party of 22nd Northumb's Regt who were working under R.A. at KEMPTON PARK. 2 boys under Major SM. Baker who were working under R.A. at KEMPTON PARK were relieved by a similar party of 19th D.L.I. and marched back to billets in SIEGE CAMP. Casualties Nil. | |

Army Form C. 2118.

# WAR DIARY
## or
## INTELLIGENCE SUMMARY.  14th (S) Bn. Glost. Regiment

(Erase heading not required.)

Instructions regarding War Diaries and Intelligence Summaries are contained in F. S. Regs., Part II. and the Staff Manual respectively. Title pages will be prepared in manuscript.

| Place | Date | Hour | Summary of Events and Information | Remarks and references to Appendices |
|---|---|---|---|---|
| Siege Camp | 29/11/17 | | The early part of the day was spent in cleaning equipment, kit etc. At about 2 pm the two companies who were relieved from Kempton Park again moved up to Turco Camp & work under R.A. Lamallin hill. | |
| Siege Camp & Kempton Park | 30/11/17 | | Companies at Kempton Park and Turco Camp working under R.A. throughout the day. Casualties 1 O.R. Wounded in action. Artillery activity throughout the day. | |

..........................................
L. P. Sloan
Lieut. Col.
Comdg. 14th (S) Bn. Gloster Regt. (W. of E.)

Army Form C. 2118.

# WAR DIARY
## of
14th (S) Bn. Gloster Regt.

## INTELLIGENCE SUMMARY.
Period 1st to 31st December 1917.

(Erase heading not required.)

Instructions regarding War Diaries and Intelligence Summaries are contained in F. S. Regs., Part II. and the Staff Manual respectively. Title pages will be prepared in manuscript.

| Place | Date | Hour | Summary of Events and Information | Remarks and references to Appendices |
|---|---|---|---|---|
| Kempton Park and Lurso Camps | 1/12/17 | | Companies were working under Royal Artillery during the day. Artillery activity along the front continued throughout the day. – Casualties Nil. | |
| - " - | 2/12/17 | | Companies were working under Royal Artillery as on previous day. At 2.30 pm the parties back from Kempton Park and Lurso Camps were relieved and marched to billets in Siege Camp. – Casualties Nil. | |
| Siege Camp | 3/12/17 | | General Training was carried out from 9am to 12.30pm including Range practices during the afternoon the Battalion attended the Baths. – Casualties Nil. | |
| - " - | 4/12/17 | | General training was carried out from 9am to 12.30pm, including instruction in Bullet & Bayonet by Army Gymnastic Instructor. Companies on Range during afternoon. – Casualties Nil. | |
| - " - | 5/12/17 | | Morning was spent in preparation for the line. In the afternoon the Battalion moved off and relieved the 9th Batt. East Yorks Regt. in the line. The relief was carried out without incident. 10 casualties. 2 O.R. Wounded. | |
| Langemarck Sector | 6/12/17 | | General improvement of Posts during the day. Patrols encountered no enemy. Casualties – Nil. | |
| - " - | 7/12/17 | | Usual artillery activity throughout the day. At night the Battalion was relieved by the 15th Sherwood Foresters & moved back to Support. Relief was carried out without incident. Patrol encountered Nil. Casualties Nil. | |

Army Form C. 2118.

# WAR DIARY
## or
## INTELLIGENCE SUMMARY.
*(Erase heading not required.)*

Commdg. 14th (S) Bn. Gloster Regt.

| Place | Date | Hour | Summary of Events and Information | Remarks and references to Appendices |
|---|---|---|---|---|
| Lancemark Sector | 8/12/17 | | Eagle Dump was shelled steadily throughout the day also Boyle Trench. At night the Battalion was relieved by the 2/10 London Regt. During the relief A Track was shelled rather heavily. Relief was carried out without further incident. Battalion marched back to Siege Camp. Casualties 4 O.R. wounded. | |
| Siege Camp | 9/12/17 | | At 9/30 am Battalion paraded and marched to Elverdinghe Station & entrained for Proven. Here the Battalion detrained and marched through the town and entrained again on Light Railway which conveyed them to Herzeele. Battn marched from Station to Billets near the village. Casualties Nil. | |
| Herzeele | 10/12/17 | | The day was spent in cleaning up of Equipment Kits &c. Inspections by Platoon Commanders. Casualties Nil. | |
| " | 11/12/17 | | Battalion moved off from Herzeele in the morning & marched to Buteh in School Camp. Casualties Nil. | |
| School Camp | 12/12/17 | | General Training was carried out between the hours of 9/30am & 12.30pm including Musketry on the Range. The afternoon was devoted to Recreation. Inter Bath. Football match played. Casualties Nil. | |
| " | 13/12/17 | | General Training commenced at 8/30am including Musketry on Range. Platoon Drill &c which continued until 12/30pm. Afternoon was devoted to General Games Sport Exercises &c. | |
| " | 14/12/17 | | General Training was carried out as on previous day. Casualties Nil. | |

A5834 Wt. W4973/M687 750,000 8/16 D.D. & L. Ltd. Forms/C.2118/13.

**Army Form C. 2118.**

# WAR DIARY
## or
## INTELLIGENCE SUMMARY.
*(Erase heading not required.)*

| Place | Date | Hour | Summary of Events and Information | Remarks and references to Appendices |
|---|---|---|---|---|
| School Camp | 15/12/17 | | General training as on previous day. Bombing & Lewis Gunners training under respective officers. Protective measures against hostile aircraft were elaborated. Casualties Nil. | |
| " | 16/12/17 | | Church of England Parade Service was held on football ground in the morning. Musketry on Ranges. Brigade League Football match won & drawn in the afternoon. Casualties Nil. | |
| " | 17/12/17 | | Inspection by Platoon & Company Commanders. Training in Musketry & Bayonet fighting with inclusive instructors. Communication Drill for NCOs during the morning. Afternoon was devoted to General Sports. Football &c. Casualties Nil. | |
| " | 18/12/17 | | Training carried out as on previous day including Range practice. Casualties Nil. | |
| " | 19/12/17 | | General training was carried out between the hours of 9/30 am & 12/30pm including Musketry on Range. The afternoon was devoted to inter Batt. Football. Casualties Nil. | |
| " | 20/12/17 | | General training was carried out between the hours of 8/30 am & 12/30pm including Musketry & Running. Afternoon was devoted to General Sports. Football &c. Casualties Nil. | |
| " | 21/12/17 | | General training carried out as on previous day. Casualties Nil. | |
| " | 22/12/17 | | General training carried out between 8/30 am & 12/30pm including Musketry & Running. Inter Batt. Football match in afternoon. | |

Army Form C. 2118.

# WAR DIARY
## or
## INTELLIGENCE SUMMARY.
(Erase heading not required.)

Intelligence summary

Cmdg. 14th (S) Bn. Gloster R. BEF.

| Place | Date | Hour | Summary of Events and Information | Remarks and references to Appendices |
|---|---|---|---|---|
| School Camp | 23/12/17 | | Divine Service in Recreation Hut & the Joncey of Musketry Competition in morning afternoon. Cup Officers & Sergeants Revolver competition was held. | Casualties Nil |
| " | 24/12/17 | | During the day Events in the Brigade Sports were held - | Casualties Nil |
| " | 25/12/17 | | Voluntary Drums Service was held in the morning. Brigade Football Match in the afternoon - | Casualties Nil |
| " | 26/12/17 | | During the day events in the Brigade Sports were held - | Casualties Nil |
| " | 27/12/17 | | Events competition & Cross Country Run. The Rugby Games 2nd Prize in Cross Country Run. | Casualties Nil |
| " | 28/12/17 | | Special Training was carried out from 5/30 am to 12/30 pm. The afternoon was devoted to Recreation - | Casualties Nil |
| " | 29/12/17 | | General Training carried out as on previous day - | Casualties Nil |
| " | 30/12/17 | | Divine Service Church Parade morning. Competition in which the Battalion was shown a representative in Gas & Musketry competition for 105th Brigade | Casualties Nil |
| " | 31/12/17 | | General Training was carried out from 8/30 am to 12/30 pm. Afternoon being devoted to education. | Casualties Nil |

35/105
Army Form C. 2118.

14 GLOSTER REGT
Vol 24

# WAR DIARY
## or
## INTELLIGENCE SUMMARY.
(Erase heading not required.)

Instructions regarding War Diaries and Intelligence Summaries are contained in F. S. Regs., Part II. and the Staff Manual respectively. Title pages will be prepared in manuscript.

| Place | Date | Hour | Summary of Events and Information | Remarks and references to Appendices |
|---|---|---|---|---|
| School Camp | 1/1/18 | | General training carried out between 8.30 am & 12.30pm. Afternoon was devoted to the preparation for moving to MURAT CAMP. Casualties nil. | |
| School Camp | 2/1/18 | | Battalion marched off at 10.45am to BYNG for entrainment to TAUNTON. From there marched to MURAT CAMP. Casualties nil. | |
| Murat Camp | 3/1/18 | | Worked on posts under II Corps R.E. & 19th Northumberland Fusiliers. Casualties nil. | |
| Murat Camp | 4/1/18 | | Working parties as on previous day. About 5/30 pm enemy aircraft dropped bombs in vicinity of Gouzeaucourt — 1. Lieut F. Billington. | |
| Murat Camp | 5/1/18 | | Working Parties as on previous day. Casualties nil. | |
| Murat Camp | 6/1/18 | | Working Parties as on previous day. Casualties nil. | |
| Murat Camp | 7/1/18 | | Worked parties as on previous day. Casualties nil. | |
| Murat Camp | 8/1/18 | | Worked parties as on previous day. Casualties nil. | |

L.22

Army Form C. 2118.

# WAR DIARY
## or
## INTELLIGENCE SUMMARY.
(Erase heading not required.)

Instructions regarding War Diaries and Intelligence Summaries are contained in F. S. Regs., Part II. and the Staff Manual respectively. Title pages will be prepared in manuscript.

| Place | Date | Hour | Summary of Events and Information | Remarks and references to Appendices |
|---|---|---|---|---|
| Frigar Camp | 9/1/18 | | The morning was devoted to the preparation for movement to Burnt Bank. | Intiumatt... |
| | | 1/30 pm | Battalion marched to Burnt Bank. Casualties nil | |
| Burnt Bank | 10/1/18 | | General Fatigue Parties throughout the day in improvement of Cooks on the vicinity on Burnt Bank. Casualties nil | |
| | 11/1/18 | | General Fatigue parties as on previous day. Casualties nil | |
| Burnt Bank | 12/1/18 | | During the morning Fatigue parties were provided for Divisional Headquarters. These not finished on morning were in the afternoon for the whole Battalion. Casualties nil | |
| Burnt Bank | 13/1/18 | | General Fatigue parties to Divl Headquarters also under Arm Command, and for the filling Burnt Store was held in the morning. Casualties nil | |
| Burnt Bank | 14/1/18 | | General Fatigue Parties as on previous day. Casualties nil | |
| Burnt Bank | 15/1/18 | | General Fatigue as on previous day. Commanding officer & Company Commanders, reconnoitred the Line in preparation for relief. Casualties nil | |

# WAR DIARY
## INTELLIGENCE SUMMARY

Army Form C. 2118.

| Place | Date | Hour | Summary of Events and Information | Remarks and references to Appendices |
|---|---|---|---|---|
| Forest Rich | 11/9/18 | | Bn moved again to Forest rico, relieving the 23rd Brigade Gemach on Left and 8 Battn of the Field on the right. Relief was carried out without incident. | Intelligence |
| 1st Flesor | 12/9/18 | | Enemy shewing signs of machine gun fire worse on flanks. Ground saturated wet - Casualties: nil. | |
| " | | | Ground still intensively Enemy Artillery especially great machine Gun fire from GRAVEL FARM & MERRIS FARM. Trench mortar firing at BERTHIER FARM. Casualties 3 wounded at OR's. | |
| " | 13/9/18 | | Ground still impassable. Patrols only able to do what work between lines. Enemy artillery most active throughout the day. TAUBE FARM, A ROAD and EAGLE DUMP shelled at intervals. Casualties nil. | |
| " | 14/9/18 | | Enemy lit last our Patrols were able to gain known recent left known BROOKSEEN Area. None 1 round. Enemy Battery most active than usual TRANQUIL FARM, CONDÉ & SENEGAL shell heavily at intervals, by TT am from direction of FOOTHURST FOREST. to depth the Battalion was relieved by 18th Sherwood Foresters. Relief being carried out without incident - W X Coy CANDLE TRENCH Y & Z Coys EAGLE TRENCH Battalion HQ DOG WHISTLE Casualties nil. | |

# WAR DIARY or INTELLIGENCE SUMMARY

Army Form C. 2118.

| Place | Date | Hour | Summary of Events and Information | Remarks and references to Appendices |
|---|---|---|---|---|
| LEFT SECTOR | 21/1/18 | | EAGLE TRENCH. Slightly shelled. 5th men received Trench Foot treatment. Casualties Nil. | Intelligence nil |
| " | 22/1/18 | | Enemy Artillery quiet. All men again received Trench Foot treatment. X Ray ord Bath. Casualties Nil. | |
| " | 23/1/18 | | Enemy Artillery quiet. Salvage Pts. examined for Salvage work on Trestles. Casualties Nil. | |
| " | 24/1/18 | | At night the Battalion was relieved by the 23rd Manchester Regt & in turn moved to TURCO CAMP. Relief was carried out without incident. Casualties Nil. | |
| TURCO CAMP | 25/1/18 | | W.T. Rifles in or Working Parties. & all men received Trench foot treatment. Casualties Nil. | |
| " | 26/1/18 | | D.O. Coy of incoming regiment taking Courses were elaborated. Casualties Nil. | |
| " | 27/1/18 | | Groups carries held during the morning. Kit & equipment inspections during afternoon. Casualties Nil. | |

Army Form C. 2118.

# WAR DIARY
## or
## INTELLIGENCE SUMMARY.
*(Erase heading not required.)*

Instructions regarding War Diaries and Intelligence Summaries are contained in F. S. Regs., Part II. and the Staff Manual respectively. Title pages will be prepared in manuscript.

| Place | Date | Hour | Summary of Events and Information | Remarks and references to Appendices |
|---|---|---|---|---|
| TURCO CAMP | 28/8 | | General Fatigue Parties were supplied by Battalion for work on Roads & improvement of Camp. Casualties Nil. | |
| " | 29/8. | | As on previous day, fatigue parties were supplied, working under R.E. Casualties Nil. | |
| " | 30/8. | | Protective measures against Enemy Aircraft were carried out by various fatigue parties throughout the day. Casualties Nil. | |
| " | 31/8. | | Party attended Hampton Park for Foot treatment. General Fatigue Parties throughout the day. Casualties Nil. | |

A5834 Wt. W4973/M687 750,000 8/16 D. D. & L. Ltd. Forms/C.2118/13.

**Army Form C. 2118.**

**WAR DIARY**
or
INTELLIGENCE SUMMARY.
*(Erase heading not required.)*

14th (S) Bn. Gloster Regt

February 1918

Instructions regarding War Diaries and Intelligence Summaries are contained in F. S. Regs., Part II. and the Staff Manual respectively. Title pages will be prepared in manuscript.

| Place | Date | Hour | Summary of Events and Information | Remarks and references to Appendices |
|---|---|---|---|---|
| TURCO CAMP | 1/2/18 | | Battalion moved into front line relieving 23rd Manchester Regiment. It this was carried out without incident. Casualties - Nil. | |
| LANGEMARCK Sector | 2/2/18 | | Lieut Rough + Osborne went round our Sectors - nil. Patrols sent out. Our wire carried out. Casualties 1. O.R. wounded. | |
| " | 3/2/18 | | Quiet night. At 7pm 2nd Lieut E.T. Rundle DCM and 2nd Lieut E.W. Denby + 38 other Ranks of Z Coy. Left GRAVEL FARM. 2nd Party left TATCH FARM at 6.30 pm. + moved E along the line WATERNLIETBEEK to the S.E. of CRAVEN. The parties were divided into two equal parties, one Ben Sections carrying Bangalore Torpedoes were attached to each. W Coy supplied two platoons for front line duty, and a "Z" Coy as support. Zero 7 PM. Main message found in enemy + surrounding Pill Boxes. Two bangalores had no effect on one cott. Farm found to consist of 3 buildings connected. In front enemy found, 1 Pill Box proving full. 2nd Second S.O.S. was fired on Star Bombs + 1 German prisoner. The Bangalore exploded and killed 12 dead were lying round the building, Corpl Price supposedly killed. Dugouts to front half buried, its being destroyed with bombs. | L. 23 |

Lieut. Col. Comdg. 14th (S) Bn. Gloster Regt. (W. of E.)

Army Form C. 2118.

# WAR DIARY
## or
## INTELLIGENCE SUMMARY.
(Erase heading not required.)

Comdg. 14th (S) Bn. Gloster Regt. (W. of E.)
Lieut. Col. ..................................
E.F.S. Ford

| Place | Date | Hour | Summary of Events and Information | Remarks and references to Appendices |
|---|---|---|---|---|
| LANGEMARCK Sector | 4/3/18 | (contd) | Casualties – 4 ORs wounded. Enemy retaliation barrage being rather heavy on Support line, two casualties (both wounded) happened here. <br><br> REPORT by BRIG. GEN. MARINDIN DSO <br><br> The leading of the Raid & behaviour of all ranks appear to have been excellent. Great credit is also due to Major WASS M.C. & Cpl SHUFFLEBOTHAM M.C. for the careful way in which they organised & prepared the raid. <br><br> CONGRATULATORY MESSAGES <br><br> "Tell Col Ford Please convey my congratulations to all ranks on the excellent organisation & gallant carrying out of the Raid." <br><br> BRIG GEN MARINDIN. DSO. <br><br> "WDT Bn. Commander congratulates WDT on Successful Raid." <br><br> "As Corps Com. under orders wishes you to convey to Brig Gen MARINDIN DSO and and R of WDT his congratulations on successful raid carried out last night. I am personally glad that the 14th Gloucesters have had the opportunity of showing the enemy as in bygone old times on Flanders, he cannot be caught out." | |

# WAR DIARY
## or
## INTELLIGENCE SUMMARY.

(Erase heading not required.)

Army Form C. 2118.

Comdg. 14th (S) Bn. Gloster Regt. (W. of E.)
Lieut. Col. ......................

E. S. Pearl

| Place | Date | Hour | Summary of Events and Information | Remarks and references to Appendices |
|---|---|---|---|---|
| LANGEMARCK Sector | 5/2/18 | | The Battalion was relieved by 15th Sherwood Foresters. Y + W Coys to EAGLE TRENCH. Z + X Coys to SOULT CAMP. Headquarters to PIG + WHISTLE. Casualties Nil. | |
| Soult Camp | 6/2/18 | | During the day Z + X Coys were employed cleaning up preparatory to departure for 13th Gloucester Regt. Y + W Coys to Westerning Parade. Casualties Nil. | |
| Eagle Trench | 7/2/18 | | Y + W Coys on Working Parade. Casualties 1 OR wounded. | |
| Eagle Trench | 8/2/18 | | Y + W Coys relieved by the 15th Cheshire Regt. The Companies endeavoured for T Camp. | |
| T Camp | 9/2/18 | | In the morning Z + X Coys marched to T camp. On Show the Battalion was inspected by Corps Commander. | |
| T Camp | 10/2/18 | | Divine Service and Bible and in the morning, the remainder of the day being spent in preparation for Divine days march. | |

# WAR DIARY
## or
## INTELLIGENCE SUMMARY.

(Erase heading not required.)

Army Form C. 2118.

Instructions regarding War Diaries and Intelligence Summaries are contained in F.S. Regs., Part II. and the Staff Manual respectively. Title pages will be prepared in manuscript.

Comdg. 14th (S) Bn. Gloster Regt. (W. of E.)
Lieut. Col. ..................
L.B.S. Fand

| Place | Date | Hour | Summary of Events and Information | Remarks and references to Appendices |
|---|---|---|---|---|
| J. Camp | 11/5/16 | | 12 Officers, 250 Rankers transferred to 13th Gloucester Regt. Remainder of Battalion marched to PROVEN & entrained for BOLLEZEELE to lay detention & marched to Suffolk lines II Corps Reinforcement Camp. | |
| BOLLEZEELE | 12/5/16 | | The morning was spent to General Training. During the afternoon accessive fatigue parties were employed on improvement of Camp. | |
| | 13/5/16 | | Working parties were provided for work at POLO Camp MERCKEGHEM. The remainder of Coy. on General Training including Range practice. | |
| | 14/5/16 | | Fatigue & General Training as on previous day. | |

www.ingramcontent.com/pod-product-compliance
Lightning Source LLC
Chambersburg PA
CBHW081549160426
43191CB00011B/1880